DESIGNING AND EVALUATING

Games and and Simulations

Gulf Publishing Company
Houston, London, Paris, Zurich, Tokyo

DESIGNING

AND

EVALUATING

Games

and

Simulations

A Process Approach

● ● ● ● ● ● ● ●

Margaret Gredler

This edition published in 1994 by Gulf Publishing
Company, Houston, under special arrangement with
Kogan Page, London.

Gulf Publishing Company
Book Division
P.O. Box 2608 • Houston, Texas 77252-2608

10   9   8   7   6   5   4   3   2   1

Library of Congress Cataloging-in-Publication Data

Gredler, Margaret E.
   Designing and evaluating games and simulations : a
process approach / Margaret Gredler.
      p.   cm.
   Includes index.
   ISBN 0-88415-157-3
   1. Educational games—Design and construction.
2. Simulation games in education—Design and
construction.   3. Educational games—Evaluation.
4. Simulation games in education—Evaluation.
I. Title.
LB1029.G3G67   1994
371.3′078—dc20   93-30548
                                                      CIP

Printed in the United States of America.

Contents

Preface

Games and simulations are experiential activities that have gained acceptance in classrooms at all levels of education and training and in a variety of subject areas. However, at present several key questions about design and evaluation remain unanswered. Among them are, what are the essential process characteristics that differentiate simulations from other interactive activities? What are the process flaws in computer-managed exercises that prevent them from being effective simulations? How do simulations in which the focus is data management and interpretation differ from those that are propelled by human interactions? What are the process characteristics essential in evaluating games and simulations for use in classrooms?

This book proposes factors to be considered in answering these and other questions about games and simulations. The analyses presented are based on the types of events that precipitate learner actions, the types of actions or behaviours that receive reinforcement, the nature of feedback for the individual's actions, and the relationship of the individual to others in the exercise. These process characteristics differentiate games and simulations and also differentiate data-management and social-process simulations. They indicate also the richness and diversity of well-designed games and simulations for education.

1 A relational model of games and simulations

Interactive group exercises became a curriculum staple in education and training in the 1960s. To date, however, comprehensive design guidelines that differentiate the various types of interactive exercises and which are easy to use are lacking. One recently-developed taxonomy of simulations, for example, includes over 90 categories and sub-categories. Of importance to designers and potential users of games and simulations are definitive criteria that reflect the key processes operating in each type of exercise.

NEED FOR A COMPREHENSIVE THEORY

The need for a comprehensive analysis of interactive exercises is indicated by two current problems. One is the negative effects of poorly-developed exercises. This problem is particularly apparent in microcomputer exercises. For example, some computer exercises that are labelled 'simulations' are merely drill-and-practice exercises accompanied by animated graphics (Gredler, 1986).

Others are Russian-roulette types of exercises that purport to 'simulate' such events as operating a lemonade stand. However, the only activity executed by students is the assignment of values to a few variables in an effort to guess the 'correct' values acceptable to the computer program. The curriculum message embedded in such exercises is that ability and hard work do not influence life outcomes. Instead, success is random.

The second major problem in accurately analysing interactive exercises is the inconsistent application of the terms 'games' and 'simulations'. One typical result is that some participants view an exercise as a game and others treat it as a simulation (Jones, 1987). An example is a phenomenon observed in business simulations (typically referred to as 'games'). These exercises involve several rounds or cycles of business or trading. Sometimes a business team that is not doing well in later rounds attempts to 'crash the system' (Lundy, 1985). These participants are behaving like game players and, seeing no way to 'win', behave in such a way as to prevent others from 'winning'. Their behaviour, of course, ruins the experience for the other participants.

The inconsistent use of the terms 'games' and 'simulations' leads to the mixing of techniques that seriously flaws an exercise (Jones, 1987). A common practice is the use of scoring criteria or other mechanisms of determining winners and losers in exercises that purport to reproduce a particular psychological reality.

An example is the *Life Career Game* developed in the 1960s. Teams of 2–4 players, using the profile of a fictitious person, planned the individual's schedule of school activities, job, family responsibilities and leisure for 1 week (1 round) up to 12 weeks or rounds. Points were assigned for different decisions about education, occupation, family life and leisure.

Such decisions, however, are value-laden; that is, they depend in large measure on one's basic philosophy of life and personal goals. To score such decisions as though they were 'right' or 'wrong' in the same way that statements about geography or biology are either right or wrong is to distort the basic decision-making process. A participant cannot totally focus on making decisions consistent with his or her belief system when the bottom line is a total score. In other words, to mix social processes with efforts to score points leads to confusion, unintended side effects and a reduction in the effectiveness of the exercise.

Similar effects also occur with the use of the categories that join the two terms, ie, 'gaming-simulation' and 'simulation-gaming'. Games and simulations represent different psychological realities. Thus, merging the two categories results in a contradiction in terms and the exercises send conflicting messages to participants (Jones, 1984; 1987). Gaming-simulations also can lead to bad feelings between participants who address their roles in a professional manner and those who treat the exercise as 'only a game'. To mix the two categories, in other words, is like mixing oil and water (Jones, 1987).

One reason for the confusion in terminology is that interactive exercises often are categorized according to surface characteristics such as the various types of paraphernalia that are used (eg, boards, role cards, tokens, etc.). Instead, games and simulations should be analysed in terms of their fundamental defining features, or 'deep structure' (van Ments, 1984). For the purpose of analysis in this text, deep structure is further defined as the nature of the interactions (a) between participants and the situation, crisis, problem or task, and (b) among participants in the exercise (Gredler, 1990, p. 329). Analysis of deep structure includes identification of the types of objects and events that precipitate learner actions, the types of actions or behaviours that earn reinforcement, the nature of feedback for the individual's actions, and the relationship of the individual to others in the exercise. This approach is used in the text to differentiate between games and simulations and to identify key differences between types of simulations (discussed later in this chapter).

BASIC DEFINITIONS

Both games and simulations are interactive exercises. However, each fulfils a separate purpose and establishes a particular psychological situation for the player (game) or participant (simulation).

Games

A commonly-accepted definition of a game is that it is 'any contest (play) among adversaries (players) operating under constraints (rules) for an objective (winning, victory, pay-off)' (Abt, 1968). The difficulty with this definition is the use of the word 'contest'. That is, contests encompass two types of activities, only one of which is a game. Specifically, some contests are engaged in for fun, entertainment, or simply to exercise one's skill. A variety of activities from competitive exercises on the playing field to intellectual contests, such as bridge, chess, or backgammon, are in this group. Although consequences are experienced by the players within the exercise, the consequences do not apply to real-life outcomes.

In contrast, other contests are serious and important events in one's life that may be accompanied by long-term implications. Examples include licensing examinations in various fields such as medicine or law, competitions for scholarships and similar events (Jones, 1987). They are not engaged in for fun or entertainment. Thus, to describe a game as a contest fails to address the essence of the activity.

Three important characteristics define a competitive exercise as a game. First, a game is a world unto itself that is determined by its own particular sets of rules that are not replications of real life. Moreover, the consequences experienced as a player in a game do not extend to real life. Losing all one's money in *Monopoly*, for example, does not lead to being declared bankrupt in one's daily affairs.

Second, the paraphernalia used in a game and the consequences prescribed by the rules may be any of a vast combination of objects and events that may enable a player or a team to defeat one's opponents. Several athletic games, for example, make use of any of several odd-shaped balls and implements (small balls, large balls, pucks, sticks, bats, mallets, paddles, rackets and so on) and a set of rules for setting the projectile in motion and earning points or penalties. Board games, in contrast, use carved figures, pegs, marbles, small round discs and other markers that are manipulated in various ways in allocated spaces on the board.

Third, a game involves winning by taking any course of action allowed by the rules to thwart or defeat other players. In bridge, for example, when one team wins the bid or contract, the objective of the other team is to prevent them from capturing enough cards (tricks) to meet their contract.

Sometimes the behaviours sanctioned in a game are considered reprehensible in the real world. In *Monopoly*, for example, players are reinforced for adding hotels to properties and charging high rents. The objective is to bankrupt the other players. In the real world, of course, bankrupting one's colleagues would be considered the epitome of greed. Thus, it is important to remember that any game is a fantasy world, defined by its particular rules and efforts to win within those rules.

Simulations

The term 'simulation' has been used in a variety of ways. Included are efforts to model some complex process or reality, and a representation of some aspect of the universe. However, modelling or imitating the central features of a situation does not render an activity a simulation. The question is, what types of actions are the participants engaged in and what kinds of decisions are they making?

Suppose, for example, a group of students is given a portfolio of materials describing the terrain, natural resources, towns and industries of a seaside region in a small country. The students are asked to plan a viable energy policy for the region for the next decade.

In this exercise, the students are taking part in a group problem-solving activity that makes use of simulated materials. Of course, a simulation is a problem-based exercise. However, a simulation differs from a group planning exercise in several ways. First, a specific issue, problem or policy is posed that precipitates a variety of actions by the participants. In other words, some precipitating or initiating event to which participants react is a key characteristic of simulations. An example is a proposal to build a nuclear reactor on the coast near the town.

Second, roles are defined that interact with the posed problem or issue in particular ways. In a simulation about a proposed nuclear reactor, the roles would likely include the mayor of the seaside town, the head of the local environmental group, various government officials promoting different energy policies, and so on. In addition to each participant receiving a description of his or her role, all receive a copy of a press release announcing that the government is considering building a nuclear reactor near the town. The participants then interact in their various positions in response to the press release as they attempt to meet their goals and priorities.

This brief description illustrates two major criteria of simulations. First, a simulation involves the experience of functioning in a bona fide role and encountering the consequence of one's actions as one makes decisions in the execution of that role. Second, the participants address the issues and problems seriously and conscientiously, ie, in a professional manner (Jones, 1984). This critical feature of simulations is referred to by Jones (1984; 1987) as 'reality of function'. That is, 'a chairman really is a chairman with all the power, authority, and duties to complete the task' (Jones, 1984, p 45).

Reality of function refers to more than the words or actions of the participants – it also includes their thoughts (Jones, 1982, p 4). In other words, participants must mentally accept the function that is expected of them in the simulation.

Developing a simulation which supports reality of function requires attention to three aspects of design. One is to establish bona fide roles for the participants in which they are to carry out important tasks that are functional in the particular social microcosm. Examples include attempting to find food and water after landing on a desert island, attempting to design the best widget, or serving as an emissary to another country. The second is to provide sufficient documentation on an issue or a problem (such as memos, newspaper articles and maps) so that the participants can behave in a professional manner (Jones, 1987, p 91). The third requirement is that of designing the simulation so that behavioural contingencies support the conscientious execution of the assigned role by the participant. That is, random behaviours or actions that are counter to the context of the exercise, such as crashing the system in a financial management exercise, are not reinforced by success.

These three requirements are of particular importance in the analysis of computer-based exercises. An example is *Lemonade Stand*, described by the developers as a simulation. Students enter values (for each 'day') for the number of glasses of lemonade to be sold, the price per glass and the daily expenditure for advertising. The computer program, using a model unrelated to the professional experience of operating a lemonade stand, calculates the daily profit or loss.

Reality of function for the participant is lacking in the exercise. First, a bona fide role in a meaningful social context is not established. The participant is not informed as to whether the role is that of children or teenagers planning to earn extra money or some other situation. Further, is the stand to be located in a neighbourhood, near a school or athletic event, or some other site? In addition, the student makes repeated decisions only about three events. Other decisions such as the specific ingredients to be used in the lemonade are omitted.

The unstated goal of this exercise is for the student to discover the optimum values to be allocated to the selected variables according to the computer model (Gredler, 1989). In other words, the student interacts with the computer (the major 'player' in the exercise) rather than with an evolving scenario (Edens and Gredler, 1990). Thus, the exercise lacks reality of function. At best, it is a type of game in which the goal is to beat the computer.

In summary, five major characteristics describe simulations. They are as follows:

- Simulations are problem-based units of learning that are set in motion by a particular task, issue, policy, crisis, or problem. The problems to be addressed by the participant may be either implicit or explicit, depending on the nature of the simulation.
- The subject matter, setting and issues inherent in the simulation are *not* textbook problems or questions in which answers are cut-and-dried and determined quickly.
- Participants carry out functions associated with their roles and the settings in which they find themselves.
- The outcomes of the simulation are *not* determined by chance or luck. Instead, participants experience consequences that follow from their own actions.
- Participants experience reality of function to the extent that they fulfil their roles conscientiously and in a professional manner, executing all the rights, privileges and responsibililties associated with the role.

MAJOR TYPES OF SIMULATIONS

The prior criteria provide general guidelines for evaluating potential exercises for classroom use. However, in designing simulations, the possibilities for different kinds of interactions between participants and issues as well as interactions with each other at first seem almost endless.

Nevertheless, simulations may be categorized into major types and groups based on the general nature of the dynamics of the interactions produced by the simulation. In other words, attempting to categorize simulations as 'business simulations', 'social simulations', 'computer simulations' and so on does not reveal the underlying dynamics of the particular exercise. Such a categorization is referred to by van Ments (1984, p 52) as 'surface structure'.

Instead, simulations should be examined in terms of their fundamental defining features or 'deep structure' (van Ments, 1984). As stated earlier, identifying the nature of the interactions in the exercise reveals different types of simulations.

For example, in one simulation, members of an archeological team sift through the soil of a constructed dig and analyse the discovered fragments. The goal is to determine the nature of an ancient civilization. In contrast, in another simulation, the participants are pupils faced with impossible tasks in their classroom. By the end of the exercise, the participants have experienced frustration, humiliation and anger.

These two simulations differ in the types of tasks established for the participants and the nature of the interactions in the particular exercise (deep structure). As a result, the participants focus on different kinds of goals and undergo different kinds of experiences. In the first example, the primary interactions are with a complex problem in which participants, in executing their roles, make use of their skills in interpreting data, organizing their findings and managing a solution strategy to the problem. This simulation is one of several exercises referred to as *tactical-decision simulations*.

In contrast, the latter example is a simulation in which the participants attempt to function as members of a social group, in this case, an elementary school classroom. In this example, the participants experience the same frustrations and emotional reactions often experienced by learning–disabled pupils. This exercise is one type of the group of simulations referred to as *social-process simulations*. The primary interactions in such simulations are between and among participants as they attempt to achieve particular social or political goals.

Table 1.1 *Key characteristics of tactical-decision and social-process simulations*

COMPONENT	TACTICAL-DECISION SIMULATIONS	SOCIAL-PROCESS SIMULATIONS
a. Task established for the participants	To interact with a complex evolving problem or crisis and bring it to a safe and/or logical conclusion	To interact with other members of a social group or groups in an effort to achieve a particular social or political goal or to address a particular challenge
b. Focus of participant attention	An evolving scenario of a complex problem or crisis that depends on data interpretation and management for resolution	Actions executed by other participants and the effects on one's own assumptions, goals, and strategies
c. Role of problems in the situation	Explicit – they are the 'raison d'être' of the simulation	Implicit – they arise from conflicting participant goals or actions
d. Participant actions essential for success	Perceiving, interpreting and organizing data, implementing strategies derived from the data interpretation	Use of various types of social communication, including interviewing, writing, editing, persuasion, negotiation, confrontation, etc.
e. Primary form of feedback to participants	Changes in the nature or status of the problem	Reactions of other participants

Table 1.1 summarizes the major characteristics of these two broad categories of simulations. As indicated, they differ in a) the basic task established for the participants, b) the focus of participant attention, c) the role of problems in the simulation, d) activities essential for participant success, and e) the primary form of reactions to participant actions.

The four components illustrated in Table 1.1 illustrate the nature of the deep structure for these two major categories of simulations. In other words, a basic assumption of simulation development is that one can rarely, if ever, create a simulation in which perceiving, interpreting and organizing data and developing strategies from the data is equally important as using various types of social communication to achieve one's goals. (*Inter-nation Simulation*, which was based on several years' research and the development of detailed data indices on the effects of one's actions approximated, but did not achieve equal status for both functions.) Therefore, a successful simulation depends, in part, on the consistency with which the set of components is developed.

Of course, a simulation in which the major purpose is data interpretation and management in a particular role does not rule out social interaction. Members of a bank management team or a team investigating an air accident, for example, must communicate with each other. The important point, however, is that the pivotal focus of participant activity and feedback is, respectively, the changing status of the bank's resources or the progress of the accident investigation.

Tactical-decision simulations

The earliest examples of tactical-decision simulations are war games in which opposing commanders matched their forces to achieve a military objective. First used for training in 1664, these exercises have become a staple in both strategy planning and training.

However, the process of data interpretation and resource allocation to solve a problem or crisis is not limited to military exercises. At present, three types of tactical-decision simulations may be identified. They are diagnostic simulations, crisis-management simulations, and data-management simulations. Each reflects a particular type of data interpretion and management. They also differ in the basic context in which these skills are to be executed, ie, a complex, evolving problem, an impending crisis, or the ongoing management of financial or economic resources (see Table 1.2).

Several skills are required in tactical-decision simulations. They are the selection of data to provide clues to the problem or crisis, interpretation of the data, implementation of a strategy to resolve the situation and monitoring and adjusting the strategy when necessary.

Several factors are involved in establishing a situation in which participants may experience reality of function. The simulation must

Table 1.2 *Types of tactical-decision simulations*

TYPE	FOCUS	EXAMPLES
Diagnostic	Participant(s) collect data and define the nature or crux of a complex problem and implement strategies based on the interpretations of the data	
Client-management	Participant takes the role of a teacher, school psychologist, physician, or other professional and diagnoses and manages the problems of a student, patient, or other client	Any of a variety of patient or client management simulations in the health sciences, social work, or other fields
'Solve the mystery'	Participant(s) determine the causes of a particular event and/or devise a solution to or escape from the problem	*In the Hot Seat* (aircraft accident investigation)
Crisis management	Participants allocate resources in an effort to avert or minimize an impending threat or danger to a business, social service, industry, or a social, economic or political system	*Atlantis* (disaster management simulation)
Data management	Participant(s) manage a set of data in an effort to fulfil established goals, typically to improve the status of an institution or an individual	*On the Campaign Trail*

be designed so that the participant conscientiously takes on the assigned role; becomes involved with the particular problem; carefully selects and attends to relevant data; and weighs alternatives as though his or her life or career depended on the decisions.

Diagnostic simulations
Two key features characterize diagnostic simulations. First, participants in their assigned roles face a sketchy description of a multi-faceted problem. Second, in executing their roles, they seek additional data to determine the nature of the problem and then implement strategies to resolve the situation.

Two sub-types are included in this category. One is the client-management simulation in which the focus is on diagnosing and treating the problem of a particular client. The majority of examples are found in the medical field in the training and assessment of medical interns, nurses and therapists. However, the model is also appropriate for social work, counselling, educational administration and others.

The second sub-type is the 'Solve the mystery' simulation. An example is *In The Hot Seat* (Rolfe and Taylor, 1984) in which the participants are members of an accident investigation team assigned to a particular air crash. However, one as yet untapped use of this type is in subject areas such as history, literature, chemistry and others. In such an exercise the participant may take the role of a well-known literary, historical or scientific figure and attempt to solve a mystery in that field.

In both types of diagnostic simulation, the participant(s) address a situation for which they must deduce the exact nature of the problem and resolve it. Data-gathering consistent with one's role and data analysis and interpretation follow.

Also important, of course, is that elements which impinge on the problem-solving efforts of the participants intrude during the simulation. Complications in the patient's condition (client-management) and intrusions by the press and public pressure for information (accident investigation) are examples.

Crisis-management simulations

Unlike diagnostic simulations, crisis-management simulations are precipitated by a scenario that sketches an imminent crisis or a natural or industrial disaster at the community, regional, national or international level. Typically, crisis-management simulations run in real time from two to seven days.

The focus in crisis-management simulations is the interpretation of data and allocation of resources to avert, alleviate or terminate a threatening or dangerous situation. An example is *Atlantis* (Ritchie, 1985) which addresses the problem of crisis analysis and resource management in a natural or nuclear disaster. Participants assess the situation and deploy various forms of rescue, relief and repair resources. They experience the consequences of their actions in the form of data on rates of infection, numbers of dead and injured and so on.

Reality of function in crisis-management exercises is established in several ways. First, the crisis must threaten the decision-makers in the simulation. Second, they must face incomplete information and accelerated time pressures for decision-making. Third, events provided in the simulation should create the impression that, in the absence of key decisions, the situation is a runaway train that will end in disaster.

Data-management simulations

The task in a data-management simulation is to allocate economic resources to any of several variables in order to achieve a particular goal. The long-range goal is to improve the status of an institution, group or individual. A forerunner of data-management simulations developed in the 1960s is *The Sumerian Game*, set in Mesopotamia in 3500 BC. The student assumed the role of Luduga I, priest-king of Lagash, and managed the annual grain harvest for several years (Carlson, 1969).

Problems faced by the ruler included granary fires, floods, an expanding population and the needs of foreign trade. In the second phase of the exercise, the goal was to accumulate surplus supplies of grain in order to support the development of crafts and other activities.

Team simulations in data-management may also be developed. Such exercises are common in business schools in banking, finance and company management. However, they may also be used in other subject areas in which teams construct a database that they then apply to solve a particular problem.

Social-process simulations

The focus in tactical-decision simulations is an evolving problem that depends on data interpretation and management for a solution. In contrast, the focus in social-process simulations is the various human interactions involved in pursuing social or political goals. Thus, participants function as members of some group, such as villagers threatened by the imminent construction of a nuclear power plant, radio broadcasters preparing a news programme, or learning–disabled children attempting to cope in the classroom setting. Participants, in their roles, attempt to complete an assigned task in a social milieu. Actions executed by other participants and their reactions to one's own behaviour in the assigned role are key factors in planning and executing goal-implementation strategies.

The range of strategies initiated in social-process simulations includes interviewing, writing, questioning, editing, negotiation, persuasion, confrontation and others. As participants attempt to achieve their social or political goals, they may experience frustration, pride, rejection, acceptance, cooperation, conflict, anger and other emotions. Therefore, essential components of social-process simulations are the post-simulation activities. Origins of emotional reactions are explored and discussed as well as the relationships to the larger sphere of human experience.

Three types of simulation are found in this broad category. Summarized in Table 1.3, they are social system, language skills/communication and empathy/insight simulations. They differ primarily in the types of interactive processes that are set in motion in each.

Social-system simulations
The focus in social-system simulations is the complex supporting fabric of relations that is found in organized societies. The two sub-

Table 1.3 *Types of social-process simulations*

TYPE	FOCUS	EXAMPLES
Social system	Participants engage in the dynamic social and/or political processes that form the fabric of organized social groups	
Multi-agenda	Participants in different roles attempt to fulfil different political or social goals	*Inter-nation simulation St Philip*
Single-agenda	Participants, as members of a group, experience a particular process or mechanism in the social system that contradicts their accepted assumptions and/or expectations	*The Numbers Game Talking Rocks*
Language skills/ communication	Participants are placed in a challenging situation that is language-intensive; participants stretch their communication and language skills to meet the challenge	*Radio Covingham Space Crash*
Empathy/insight	Participants undergo a frustrating or traumatic event and struggle to function in the negative condition	*Me the Slow Learner*

types, multi-agenda and single-agenda simulations, differ in the range of processes that are addressed and the nature of the contingencies for participant behaviour.

In multi-agenda simulations, participants assume individual roles in a hypothesized social group and experience the complexity of establishing and implementing particular goals within the fabric established by the system. The differences and potential conflicts among the roles set in motion the dynamics of the simulation. Examples are *Inter-nation Simulation* and *St Philip*.

In *Inter-nation Simulation*, participants functioned as representatives of hypothetical nations, members of an international organization and producers of the World Newspaper. In each 70-minute cycle (one year), military alliances, trade agreements, economic treaties and other activities were undertaken. Decision-makers were constantly faced with diverse events within their broad areas of responsibility, illustrating the difficulty of mediating on several fronts simultaneously.

St Philip, in contrast, is situated in a hypothetical Caribbean island. Participants assume names and roles of members of parliament (different parties), hotel developers and private secretaries to the MPs. The conflicting issues of the development of tourism and harming the environment and way of life of the island are analogous to a variety of contemporary situations (Walford, 1983).

The single-agenda simulation, in contrast, sets up a situation in which participants as a group experience a particular social mechanism or process that contradicts typical assumptions and expectations. Examples are *The Numbers Game* and *Talking Rocks* developed by Robert F. Vernon (Jones, 1982). In *The Numbers Game*, participants experience the effects of a shift in classroom structure from a competitive to a cooperative organization. Participants in *Talking Rocks* experience the difficulties of constructing messages of important survival information for others in the absence of a written language system.

In single-agenda simulations, participants do not assume individual roles. Instead, they undergo a particular experience as members of a group. Participants in *The Numbers Game* are members of classroom teams that are each given specific problems to solve. In *Talking Rocks*, participants are a primitive group referred to as 'the Eagle people'.

Language skills/communication simulations
A key skill in functioning effectively in society is that of using language to communicate with others. The major purpose of language skills/ communication simulations is to establish interesting and involving tasks such that students engage in communication 'in spite of themselves'. Depending on the particular simulation, opportunities are provided to practise different skills, such as interviewing, reporting, note taking, drafting, editing, presenting a case, listening, negotiating and so on.

Particularly important in designing these simulations is that the task or situation established for the participants is one that is all-absorbing. Two examples are *Radio Covingham* (Jones, 1984) and *Space Crash* (Jones, 1982). In the former, participants produce and broadcast a brief news programme. Preparation takes place while items continue to be received at the station and while participants are under pressure to observe a 10-minute time limit for the broadcast.

In contrast, *Space Crash* is an imaginative simulation in which six crew members must communicate with each other in order to survive. Each role card describes vital information for survival on the planet Dy – information that is not known to the other participants. Thus, effective communication and discussion are essential skills in the simulation.

In other words, in this type of simulation, language skills are a critical means to accomplish an interesting and challenging goal. As participants become involved in the ongoing activities, they stretch their capabilities to meet the challenge.

Empathy/insight simulations

The issue of simulation characteristics that specifically contribute to the development of empathy is a relatively new one in simulation design. Requirements for developing empathy include a) placing participants in a frustrating, traumatic, or debilitating situation that evokes the feelings and frustrations experienced by a particular group and b) constructing post-simulation activities to process the feelings and emotions.

An example is *Me The Slow Learner* (Thatcher, 1983) in which prospective or in-service teachers are learning–disabled pupils in a classroom. They are fitted with different handicaps and then are allowed 24 minutes to complete 6 tasks. However, the tasks are constructed to be nearly impossible. The participant reactions during the exercise typically begin with disbelief, followed by efforts to try their best and finally apathy or rebellion.

Three issues are crucial in the decision to implement an empathy/insight simulation. They are 1) the construction of the exercise so that participants are not tricked in any way; 2) the rationale for implementing the exercise; and 3) the post-simulation activities. In other words, because these simulations generate negative emotions, they should only be used when they can reflect pivotal factors that may influence participants' decisions in working with others. Also, post-simulation discussions and other activities are essential for working through the negative emotions generated by the exercise and in developing empathy.

Discussion

The major groups of simulations introduced in this chapter reflect two different perspectives on developing meaningful problem-based exercises that require the execution of particular roles. In tactical-decision simulations, social pressures and requirements for communication are held to a minimum so that students can apply the data interpretation, organization and management required in particular roles. In contrast, the social-process simulations include the major types of simulations that address some aspect of task implementation in a social milieu. The focus in these exercises is on the factors in the social setting that a) may hamper realization of one's goals, and b) may not function in a way that is consistent with our assumptions and expectations. For example, participants in *St Philip* typically learn that 'prepared "blue-print" answers are rarely effective' in resolving complex social issues (Walford, 1983, p 170).

The purpose of these categories is to identify effective types of simulations, their characteristics and the major requirements for design. They also serve as a standard against which to analyse and evaluate already-developed exercises.

OVERVIEW OF THE TEXT

Games and simulations are two useful types of interactive exercises in the classroom. Others include role playing, microworlds and individual or group problem-solving exercises with simulated materials. The purposes, characteristics and some examples of these interactive exercises are discussed in the text.

Chapters 2 and 3 discuss academic games. Important criteria with examples of game re-design and suggestions for game development are discussed in Chapter 2. Additional issues are important, however, in computer games, because the computer is both the deliverer and the control mechanism for the exercise. These issues are discussed in Chapter 3.

Tactical-decision simulations are addressed in Chapters 4, 5, 6 and 7. Chapter 4 discusses the common characteristics of and design issues related to tactical-decision simulations. Chapter 5 describes diagnostic simulations. Characteristics and requirements for designing client-management and 'Solve the mystery' sub-types are discussed.

Chapter 6 addresses crisis-management simulations. Included are the definitions of crisis situations, characteristics of crisis-management simulations and mechanisms for maintaining a sense of threat and time pressure for the participants.

Data-management simulations are described in Chapter 7. Business simulations and resource-allocation simulations based in other settings, such as other countries and/or other historical periods, are described.

Social-process simulations are discussed in Chapters 8, 9 and 10. Chapter 8 describes simulations that reflect aspects of the complex supporting fabric of relations found in social groups. Both multi-agenda and single-agenda exercises are described.

Chapter 9 addresses simulations that place participants in challenging situations in which achieving one's goals depends on effective communication. Also discussed are specific uses of language that may be required in different language skills/communication simulations.

Empathy/insight simulations are described in Chapter 10. The particular characteristics essential for fostering empathy are discussed first. Also addressed are the nature of participant reactions, the post-simulation activities essential for developing empathy and the importance of weighing the cost/benefit ratio prior to implementation.

Typically, simulations are accompanied by a follow-up session referred to as 'debriefing'. Chapter 11, however, makes the case that a single session is insufficient for learning. The chapter presents two models of experiential learning and describes different configurations of post-simulation activities.

Chapter 12 addresses the differences between other interactive exercises that share some features of games and simulations. Included are role play, microworlds, problem-solving with simulated materials and the use of videodisc technology. Chapter 13 concludes the book with a comparison of experiential learning activities on four important issues. They are the role of competition, deep structure, reality of function and the role of technology.

REFERENCES

Abt, C (1968) 'Games for learning', in Boocock, S and Schild, E (eds) *Simulation Games in Learning*, 65–84, Beverly Hills, CA: Sage.

Carlson, T B (1969) *Learning Through Games* Washington, DC: Public Affairs Press.

Edens, K and Gredler, M (1990) 'A mechanism for screening microcomputer simulations', *Educational Technology*, **26**, 3, 46–8.

Gredler, M B (1986) 'A taxonomy of microcomputer simulations', *Educational Technology*, **22** 4, 7–12.

Gredler, M B (1989) 'A further analysis of computer-based simulations', *Simulation/Games for Learning*, **19**, 2, 76–81.

Gredler, M B (1990) Analysing deep structure in games and simulations, *Simulation/Games for Learning*, **20**, 3, 329–34.

Jones, K (1982) *Simulations in Language Teaching*, Cambridge: Cambridge University Press.

Jones, K (1984) 'Simulations versus professional educators', in Jaques, D and Tipper, E (eds) *Learning for the Future with Games and Simulations*, 45–50, Loughborough: SAGSET, Loughborough University of Technology.

Jones, K (1987) *Simulations: A Handbook for Teachers and Trainers*, London: Kogan Page.

Lundy, J (1985) 'The effects of competition in business games', in van Ments, M and Hearnden, K (eds) *Effective Use of Games and Simulation*, 199–208, Loughborough: SAGSET/Loughborough University of Technology.

Ritchie, G (1985) 'ATLANTIS: The basis for management simulation development', *Simulation/Games for Learning*, **15**, 1, 28–42.

Rolfe, J and Taylor, F (1984) '*In The Hot Seat:* An accident investigation management simulation', in Jaques, D and Tipper, E (eds) *Learning for the Future With Games and Simulations*, 149–63, Loughborough: SAGSET/Loughborough University of Technology.

Thatcher, D (1983) 'A consideration of the use of simulation for the promotion of empathy in the caring professions – "Me-The Slow Learner", a case study', *Simulation/Games for Learning*, **13**, 1, 10–16.

van Ments, M (1984) 'Simulation and game structure', in Thatcher, D and Robinson, J (eds) *Business, Health, and Nursing Education*, 51–8, Loughborough: SAGSET/Loughborough University of Technology.

Walford, R (1983) St Philip: A simulation about the development of a Caribbean island', *Journal of Geography*, July–August, 170–75.

2 Academic games

Academic games may be designed for any level of education, for any subject area and for students of any age. Types of academic games range from simple games for young children to complex strategy exercises for adults. When games are developed for the classroom setting, however, several considerations are important. They are the nature and role of academic games, criteria for game elements and methods for determining winners. Also important to the game designer are appropriate ways to adapt games developed only for entertainment for use in the classroom.

OVERVIEW

Like other games, academic games should be both challenging and fun for the players. Academic games, however, differ from other games in purpose and the concept of winning.

The nature and purpose of academic games

Players may engage in games for any of a variety of reasons. They may be to pit one's skills against those of other players, to try one's luck in a game of chance, to while away an afternoon or to enjoy the company of others. Of importance in recreational games that require strategy or some other intellectual skill is that the execution of the skill applies only to the game situation and not to events in the outside world. That is, although some games require analysis and deduction, the execution of these skills is in reference only to a particular game situation. When one is attempting to make a difficult contract in bridge, for example, deciding to collect the opponents' trump cards or delaying this action is a context-dependent conclusion; it is based on circumstances relevant only to the distribution of cards around the table. Similarly, in golf, a player's decision as to the type of club to use depends on the location of the ball (eg fairway, sand trap), and the terrain and the distance between the ball and the cup.

In contrast, academic games are so named for two reasons. First, they require specific knowledge in a defined subject area or discipline such as mathematics, history, geography, biology or literature. Second, the intellectual skills required in the game are those that are applicable beyond the game itself to the particular course content.

Within these parameters, classroom games may be used for any of four general academic purposes. They are 1) to practise and/or to refine knowledge/skills already acquired; 2) to identify gaps or weaknesses in knowledge/skills; 3) to serve as a summation or review (eg, prior to a major test); and 4) to develop new relationships among concepts and/ or principles. The game *Strategem* (Bell, 1982), for example, was developed to focus student attention on inference-level questions and to generate different study habits.

In addition to academic goals, games may be used for the purpose of rewarding students for working hard or doing well on a particular lesson. A version of *Twenty Questions* in which the task is to guess the author, historical event and so on is particularly appropriate for this purpose.

These purposes are not necessarily independent. During a game which serves as a review or summation exercise, students may also develop some new relationships among concepts and principles.

One curriculum, known as 'Teams, Games, Tournaments', makes use of team competition on a regular basis as the culminating activity for each week's class work. The teacher first forms teams of four to five members. These teams represent a cross-section of ability levels and racial/ethnic groups. The teams, through tutoring, prepare the members for participation in the weekly tournament. For the tournament, three students of comparable ability are assigned to each tournament table and receive weighted scores at the end of play, based on their relative rank. Team scores are computed by adding together the individual scores earned by each member at his or her tournament table. Thus the more the team helps the members learn, the more likely a higher team score (DeVries and Edwards, 1973).

Academic games may be used in any learning setting that addresses intellectual skills and with any population. The game *Menu Mayhem*, for instance, was designed for a workshop for school cafeteria workers and they applied rules of food arrangement, nutrition and format. In contrast, James Humphrey (1970) describes a variety of games for teaching slow learners. One, referred to as *Hot Spot* (p 95), assists children in number recognition. Pieces of paper with numbers from 1 to 10 are placed in various spots around the floor (including several with the same numbers). The teacher displays posters or transparencies with different numbers of objects on them, one at a time. The children must identify the number of objects in the illustration and then run to the correct spot on the floor.

The scope of activities that may be included in classroom games is restricted by the requirement that players demonstrate academic knowledge or skill in the game. Thus, the designer faces a major task in providing an interesting and challenging experience for the players.

In other words, merely providing an interactive exercise in which the players manipulate content or symbols is not sufficient to label the activity a 'game'. One example (referred to as a game by the authors) uses teams of students to assess the impact of a major event such as the development of an advanced rapid transit system on the city. Ratings are produced for 30 different criteria. The teams then compare their ratings with those of an expert (whose answers are also included in the exercise). The exercise is an informative activity, but it is not a game.

The concept of winning

A major characteristic of games is that they emphasize the end result. The aim is to win, and the scoring system assists in determining the outcome (Jones, 1987). When games are developed for the academic setting, however, two considerations with regard to winning are important.

First, academic games should avoid dependence on luck, chance or random search strategies in order to win. The intention is that students apply their knowledge and skill in the subject area. Rewarding performance based on luck or inappropriate behaviours devalues the academic skills that the game purports to require. (The exception to this requirement is when two or three students who have completed their assignments or seat work early are permitted to play a game in the back of the room while the others complete their work. Simple card games that combine academic skills with the 'luck of the draw' are not a problem in such situations.)

The second major requirement for academic games is that zero-sum games should not be used. In a zero-sum game, the behaviours of all players are reinforced periodically for certain actions. However, only one player or team achieves an ultimate win, whereas the other players all lose. A well-known zero-sum game is *Monopoly* in which all players are reinforced for buying property and developing it in order to collect high rents. However, some players experience long dry spells between reinforcing plays and eventually lose all their resources.

The problem with zero-sum games is that players who experience defeat, although having executed appropriate behaviours in the game, also may experience frustration and disappointment. These reactions are to be avoided in games for classroom use.

Another problem may occur with zero-sum games when students perceive that only one individual or team may win *and* that they are losing. In such a situation, some players execute random strategies instead of applying theory or content. Others may engage in efforts to 'crash' the game as well, thus ruining the experience for the other players (Lundy, 1985).

One solution to the problem of zero-sum games is to provide for several winners, eg, the team that made the least number of errors, used the best strategy and so on. Another solution is to define success in terms of earning a certain number of points. In this way, teams are playing against an external standard (reasonably established), rather than competing against each other to be the only winner.

In summary, games should provide both an academic challenge to students as well as an enjoyable experience. Games may be used for a variety of purposes in the classroom, from generating different strategies of thinking to developing new relationships among concepts and principles. Of importance in the selection or construction of games is that the game should provide various ways for teams to win.

ISSUES IN GAME DESIGN

Five major issues about structure are important in the selection or design of academic games. They are:

- the purpose of the game and the nature of the specific task(s) built into the game;
- the designation of roles;
- the scoring system;
- surface structure versus deep structure; and
- the relationship of game elements to each other.

Game tasks

Identification of the purpose (or purposes) is important because it has implications for the strategy used in the game. That is, a game designed to reward a class for hard work is more likely to use a relatively simple strategy (such as the game *Authors*) compared to a game designed to develop new relationships among concepts.

In addition to purpose (practise skills/knowledge, identify weaknesses, serve as a review, or develop new relationships among concepts and principles), the particular academic skills that the students are to demonstrate also should be clear to the game designer or potential user. For example, are the students to demonstrate their knowledge of categories by classifying items into sets or are they to predict consequences or detect errors in a project or plan?

One mechanism for clarifying the academic skills to be included in a particular game is the types of learning developed by Robert Gagné (1977; 1985). The types of learning identify the internal psychological processes associated with different academic tasks. For example, predicting consequences or detecting errors in a project or plan involves the internal processes of the selection and application of rules appropriate for the particular situation.

Two major categories of learning identified by Gagné are verbal information and intellectual skills. The process exemplified by the student in verbal information is that of recall. That is, the student reinstates in working memory particular definitions, facts, formulas, or brief verbal descriptions that were learned previously. For example, when asked the formula for salt, the student replies 'NaCl'.

In contrast, the process involved in intellectual skills is that of interacting with symbols to make decisions and/or to manipulate the subject matter. Intellectual skills are described as 'the basic and, at the same time, the most pervasive structures of formal education' (Gagné and Briggs, 1979, p 24).

Four specific skills are included in this category. They are discrimination learning, concept learning, rule learning and problem-solving. Table 2.1 describes the three skills that may be incorporated into academic games. Problem-solving, which involves the selection of a series of appropriate rules and their application to generate a solution, is difficult to include in a manual game format because the complexity of the process slows down the play.

Table 2.1 *Two categories of academic learning**

LEARNING CATEGORY	DEFINITION	EXAMPLES
Verbal information: Recall	Reinstates in working memory an item of information	State or paraphrase definitions and/or brief verbal descriptions
Intellectual skills: Discrimination learning	Respond differently to characteristics that distinguish objects or events	Match names to definitions; chemical formulas to names
Concept learning	Identify objects or events as members of a concept class	Classify authors into types of literature Classify paintings into styles or periods
Rule learning	Respond to a class of situations with a class of performances that represent a relationship	Sequentially order related items Deduce persons or events from clues Predict consequences from brief scenarios Compare/contrast categories or concepts
Problem-solving	Select from memory and appropriately apply the sets of rules to generate a problem solution	Determine the optimum car route for a trip from among several alternatives

*Summarized from Gagné (1985) and Gredler (1992)

The intellectual skills in Table 2.1 are presented in the order of increasing complexity. That is, classifying objects or events into the appropriate concept class is more complex than identifying whether two objects are the same or different. Similarly, using and applying rules is more complex than identifying examples of a concept class.

Of importance in the design (or game selection) process is the early identification of the important skills to be executed by the game players. Sometimes novice designers begin by first selecting a format, ie, a board game, card game, or computer game. However, such decisions often limit the skills that may be included in the exercise. For example, adaptations of bingo are appropriate for matching names with definitions or chemical formulas to names (discrimination learning). However, the format does not lend itself to predicting outcomes or deducing consequences. Similarly, an adaptation of rummy (or a similar card game) is restricted to classifying objects, events or famous people into categories or sequences.

Depending on the particular purpose for using a game, several skills or only one particular skill may be required of the students. The one exception is that a game should not be restricted to rote recall questions only. Instead, such questions should be combined with those that require some decision-making about the subject area. The game *Stratagem*, for example, includes questions at three levels of complexity – recall, concept learning and rule application.

In contrast, *Menu Mayhem* requires one complex skill, that of rule-using. Designed for adult cafeteria workers, the game requires the identification of errors in examples of school menus. The range includes errors in format, nutritional balance, colour and omissions in menu entries.

Role designation

Two issues are important in the selection of roles for an academic game. One is that classroom games should make use of team competition rather than competition among individuals. The purpose of an academic game is not to create 'stars'. Instead, the game should serve as a challenging and interesting experience for all the players.

Second, where possible, different roles for students should be included. For example, the game *Stratagem* is one in which two teams of 2-3 members each take turns answering questions of varying difficulty. A key factor in the play is that each team determines the amount of play money to be wagered on their ability to answer the upcoming question. The game therefore also includes a banker to handle the funds. Having such a role provides the shy or withdrawn student an opportunity to participate without placing him or her in an uncomfortable situation.

Of importance is that such roles should be functional and facilitate the game play. Also, they should not require so much of the student's attention that he or she is unable to observe and learn from the action of the game. The role of the banker for each set of teams playing *Stratagem* meets these criteria. Another role that is often functional, when several games are operating at once in the classroom, is that of score-keeper for each game.

The scoring system

Success in academic games is typically defined in terms of the number of correct answers. This criterion may be manifested in a number of ways. In adaptations of bingo, winners are determined by certain patterns of squares that are covered by markers, ie, a row, a diagonal, or a complete card. In using such a game in the classroom, play should continue until more than one winning team has been identified.

In other games, points earned contribute to a total score that determines the winners. However, under no circumstances should students or teams lose points or be otherwise penalized for wrong answers or failure to answer a question. Such a policy can lead to frustration at the very least and is also not an appropriate mechanism for modifying student behaviour.

The game *Hot Spot*, briefly described earlier, has a scoring system that punishes children for wrong answers and for behaviours unrelated to the game. Any child who is left without a spot when the children run to the numbers on the floor forfeits a point. Any child with fewer than five points at the end of the game is designated a winner. One problem with the scoring system is that a child may be left without a spot either because he or she couldn't think of the number fast enough or because he or she couldn't run fast enough to get to one of the placards before another student.

The major problem, of course, is that points should be awarded for desired behaviours and winning should be based on receiving a specified number of points. *Hot Spot* should be restructured so that the number placards are large enough for two or three children to stand on. In other words, no child should be left without a place to go. Then each child who goes to the correct placard earns one point. Finally, any child who earns a pre-specified number of points, such as 10, is a winner.

The game *Hot Spot* involves one academic skill, that of identifying the correct number of objects in a group. Games for students in upper grades and for adults, in contrast, often involve more than one academic skill and tasks or questions of varying levels of difficulty. In such situations, the scoring system should take into account the range of difficulty inherent in the subject matter. Some questions or problems are easier than others; thus, the answers to the more difficult questions should be worth more points. In *Menu Mayhem*, for example, the players earn different points depending on the importance of the detected errors. That is, a format error in the typing or composition of the menu earns one point. An unappetizing combination, such as all yellow foods, earns two points. Omissions, such as a menu that lacks a salad (or some other selection of fresh vegetables), earn three points each while a nutritional deficiency earns four points. Similarly, in *Stratagem*, the bank pays bonuses to teams for correct answers in amounts equal to, double or triple the initial wagers, depending on the difficulty level of the particular question.

One benefit for scoring on a range of difficulty is that it increases interest in the game. Students enjoy challenges and the possibility of earning additional points for correctly answering a difficult question enhances the challenge.

Surface structure versus deep structure

Surface structure refers to the sequence of events permitted by the game format. For example, at least three suggested surface structures are possible in board games (Ellington *et al.*, 1982, p 76). The board may be used as:

- a two-dimensional matrix for building patterns or structures, such as bingo or *Scrabble*;
- a pre-determined linear path or patterns of paths along which players must progress (as in *Monopoly* and *Snakes and Ladders*);
- a field for mobile, two-dimensional play, such as chess.

In contrast, the surface structure in card games is that of constructing sets. Activities include forming sets of matching elements and numerical sequences of elements.

Unlike surface structure, deep structure refers to the psychological mechanisms that explain the two levels of interaction found in games and simulations. They are the interactions among participants in the exercise, and between participants and the situation, crisis, problem, task, and so on (Gredler, 1990, p 329).

One way to determine the deep structure of any exercise is to identify the behaviours that are reinforced during implementation. In other words, what are the positive behaviours as well as undesirable or escape behaviours that are being rewarded?

In contemporary society, receiving money often strengthens (reinforces) the specific behaviour that produced it. In the game *Monopoly*, for example, acquiring property is followed by the collection of rents from unlucky players who land on the site. Although the money generated is not real, it symbolizes status in the same way as money in society. Also, it is often accompanied by increasing control of the board, ie, acquiring power. Thus, competitive behaviour in the game is likely to be strengthened by one or more of three outcomes that typically function as reinforcers. They are producing wealth, acquiring status and acquiring power.

One important reinforcer that is often overlooked in designing academic games is mastery of the environment (Skinner, 1953, p 79). Activities that require skills, such as participating in sports and engaging in crafts, are reinforced by the successful manipulation of the environment. The popularity of the Pacman video games, for example, is the one-to-one correspondence between skilfully operating the machinery and Pacman gobbling up the little spots on the screen. Of course, what is reinforcing is successful play, ie, mastery of the environment (Skinner, 1984).

The deep structure of an academic game should be one that reinforces mastery of important content and skills. Earning points or moving tokens one or more squares for correct answers and/or appropriate strategies reinforces student mastery of the subject matter.

Moreover, as already mentioned, the game should not reward inappropriate behaviours, such as cheating or bluffing. Equally important is that winning, the ultimate reinforcement, should not depend on chance or luck. Sometimes, in an effort to enhance interest, elements are introduced in an academic game that alter the desired deep structure of reinforcing only academic skills. An example is the board game *Concepts*, an adaptation of draughts. Players move their draughts to squares that match the difficulty level of each question as they answer it.

In addition, however, players are permitted to routinely capture an opponent's draughts and the game ends when one player loses all his/her draughts. Although the player with the highest score wins, players are hampered in the task of winning by losing draughts through a mechanism unrelated to their knowledge of the subject matter. (The re-design of this game element is discussed later in this chapter.)

The inter-relationship of game elements

Every game is composed of an objective to be achieved; rules of play, including constraints; and paraphernalia for executing the play, such as tokens or cards. All of these elements should function together to create an effective and efficient game. That is, the game should sustain player interest, generate involvement by all players and be easy to implement.

First, rules and constraints should be as simple as possible. Cumbersome sets of rules are difficult to remember and game play stagnates if frequent rule checks are needed. Disagreements may also result.

Second, the paraphernalia should not result in 'go through the motions' activity. For example, is movement around a board essential? Advancing a marker one square for answering questions is inefficient unless board movement provides additional problem-solving opportunities and/or bonuses at certain points in the circuit. In other words, use of a board is recommended when movement is structured for a particular purpose or when story events portrayed at various locations on the board are essential.

Third, the target population for whom the game is intended is also important. Occasionally, games may be designed for a variety of ages. The mathematics game *Tuf*, available from Avalon Hill, is appropriate for ages 9 to 19. Players roll cubes containing numbers and mathematical symbols and the goal is to form equations. Depending on the cubes that are used, the game can be played at increasing levels of sophistication. For the most part, however, academic games are designated for particular grade or age levels.

DESIGNING ACADEMIC GAMES

Texts and articles on the design of games and simulations often describe the design process as linear to a great degree. That is, objectives are stated first and subsequent steps in the development are completed one after the other. Rarely, if ever, does the design process occur in this way. Instead, one may get an idea for a creative game, make an initial selection of game elements and then reject, supplement and adjust the elements until a workable exercise is achieved.

On the other hand, the teacher may be faced with a problem or difficulty in a particular unit and decide that a game may be part of the solution. The mechanisms for game play may arise from a review of the classroom problem itself. *Menu Mayhem*, the game developed for a workshop for adult cafeteria workers, began in this way. The issue in the workshop was that of devising an interesting mechanism for the review of essential menu characteristics. This led to the idea of devising a game whereby teams of players attempt to find the errors in a set of menus.

Another example is the game *Stratagem* which was developed to refocus student attention away from the memorization of information (recall skills) and toward skills such as comparing concepts, applying rules and predicting outcomes. The resulting game utilizes few question cards at the recall level, with the majority at the concept-learning and rule-using (predicting outcomes, deducing consequences) levels.

In addition, stating the difficulty level and topic of each question on the reverse side of each question card grew out of the need to focus student attention on important thinking processes. Similarly, the mechanism for wagering a sum of play money by team members on their ability to answer the question was included to refocus student attention on realistic appraisals of their academic skills.

Once the academic skills to be executed in the game are selected, decisions about the mechanisms of play may be made. Age and experience of the players, as well as the nature of the content are important factors that interact with the game format and rules. *Stratagem*, for example, is too complex for young players. However, games that focus on one academic skill, such as classifying objects or pictures into sets, and utilize a simple format, such as collecting cards, are appropriate for children.

Selecting a format and associated paraphernalia, devising the rules, developing the scoring system and choosing the reinforcers for student behaviours are not independent steps. Rather, one typically identifies one or more game formats that will permit students to execute the selected academic skills and other game elements evolve from this decision. Once an outline of the game and the mechanics of play are completed, they should be checked against the criteria described in this chapter. Then the game is ready for field trial with actual groups of students, after which further revision is likely to be required.

Re-designing existing games

For novice designers, adapting an existing game may be a less difficult task than developing an entirely new one. Some developers suggest the use of frame games as a design mechanism (Thiagarajan and Stolovitch, 1980). A frame game is one in which new content may be loaded onto the existing surface structure.

For example, the content of rummy involves cards that vary in two dimensions, ie, suits and values. The surface structure includes rules for collecting sets of cards in the same suit on a sequence of values, or the same value in different suits. In other words, the game involves the creation of sets from elements that vary on two dimensions. This structure or 'frame' may be used, for example, to create a game such as *Literature Rummy*. In the new version, players attempt to collect sets of cards from the same period with different forms or vice versa (Thiagarajan and Stolovitch, 1980).

Two cautions are in order in the use of frame games. First, the surface structure often imposes limits on the types of academic skills that may be used in the game. Adaptations of rummy, for example, make use of the skills of classifying into sets and/or constructing a series. However, predicting outcomes, deducing consequences, and other intellectual skills are not included.

The second caution is that chance or luck is often operating in games developed originally for entertainment. Thus, the game designer should review the existing rules to determine which options may require alteration in the academic form of the game. For example, the game of rummy permits the next player to pick up cards from the discard pile. A player's success in the game is dependent both on the luck of the draw from the deck and the availability of needed cards in the discard pile. In other words, chance is an important factor in achieving success.

Nevertheless, the concept of frame games is a useful one. Many well-designed academic games may also function as frame games for which new content may be loaded on the existing structure. The re-design of rummy and *Concepts*, discussed in the following sections, are examples.

Re-design of rummy

The major issue in re-designing rummy is to reduce the element of luck or chance in drawing cards to be played. In the revised form, a deck of 64 cards is used and 13 cards are dealt to each hand. The remaining 12 cards are turned face-up in the centre of the table.

Teams of two students each play each hand. At each turn, the team draws one card from the 12-card pool and discards one. Depending on the subject area, the objective may be to build sets of pictured objects, names of authors, well-known events and so on, according to particular criteria (concept learning). The use of 12 cards that are turned face-up as the basis for drawing additional cards requires that teams assess their hands and formulate some strategy for building card sets.

Suppose, for example, that the game is to be used in an art appreciation class. Playing cards are made of prints of well-known paintings and styles. Each card includes the title of the painting, but not the name of the artist or the particular period to which the painting belongs. Four artistic periods (eg, Realism, Impressionism) may be included. Each period consists of 16 cards, 4 cards each of 4 artists.

Each team's objective is to construct sets of the paintings of one artist or of a particular period. A team may build a set of Monet's paintings, for example, or a set of Impressionist paintings (eg, Monet, Manet, Degas, Renoir). Three cards constitute a set and the team displays a set face-up as soon as it is completed. Also, during play, a team may exercise the option to play a card that matches a set already displayed by another team. The game ends when one team runs out of cards.

When a team lays down a set of three cards, one member announces the category, eg, paintings by Manet. The team to the right of the players has the option to challenge the composition of the set. If an incorrect selection has been made, the team displaying the set must withdraw the cards.

Each team scores one point for each card that is played. In addition, for card sets that reflect a particular period, teams earn four bonus points for correctly naming *all* the artists in each set they have constructed. Thus, an incentive is built into the game to go beyond simply recognizing the paintings of a particular artist. Teams that earn a minimum of 10 points are declared winners.

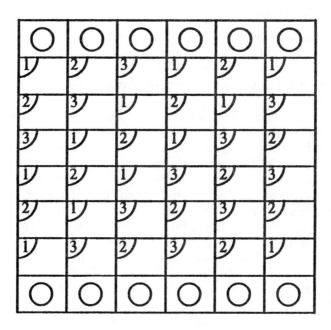

a. Pieces may move straight ahead or diagonally forward but they
   may not move backward.
b. In order to move forward, team must answer the level question
   appropriate for that square.
c. If team misses the question, the turn passes to the other team.
d. When one team's piece meets one from an opposing team they may
   elect to jump over that piece. However, the team must first
   correctly answer a level-3 question.
e. The game ends when one team has all its pieces placed in the
   'King's Row'.

Figure 2.1 *Re-design of* Concepts

The academic skill in this game is classification into sets or concept learning. Strategy rather than luck is involved in choosing cards from the available pool to complete sets and teams are reinforced for knowledge of the paintings of particular artists and periods.

Redesign of Concepts

The major issue in the redesign of *Concepts* is to eliminate the capture of a player's draughts by an opponent while retaining the challenge of the game and avoiding a 'traffic jam' of draughts in the centre of the board. Figure 2.1 illustrates the game board and the rules for the revised version.

The different levels of questions are coded by the colours blue (1), green (2) and yellow (3). A score-keeper for each game maintains the score for each team and also has access to the answers to the questions.

The intention is that several games operate in the classroom concurrently. At the end of the class period, several winners are chosen. Included are the teams that finish first, those with the most points and those with the least number of missed questions.

One disadvantage of the game, however, is the large pool of questions required for play. Of the 36 squares on the board, 12 are level-3 questions, 13 are level-2 and 11 are level-1. Thus, 24 level-3 questions are required, and they are the most difficult to write. Also, 26 level-2 and 22 level-1 questions are required. Use of the game in this format, therefore, is restricted to review before a major examination in which the intention is for students to evaluate their proficiency on several different levels of knowledge. Also, a large pool of questions may be generated both for the game and for the examination.

The redesign of rummy and *Concepts* described in this section preserves the challenge in each game while removing the element of chance in game play. Moreover, both games require important academic skills and may be used in a variety of subject areas.

In summary, academic games should be challenging and fun for the players and should utilize important intellectual skills in the particular subject area. Careful attention to scoring, the concept of winning in the classroom and the bases for reinforcement can create interesting and useful classroom games.

EVALUATING GAMES FOR THE CLASSROOM

Step 1: Determine the purpose and academic tasks in the game.
- What is the basic purpose of the game? (To practise skills/ knowledge, identify weaknesses, serve as a review, develop new relationships among concepts and principles or to reward a class for hard work?)

- Are intellectual skills required in the game? If so, which ones? (Discrimination learning, concept learning or rule learning.)
- For what age group or grade level is the game designed?

Step 2: Identify player roles in the game.
- Does the game use team competition rather than individual competition?
- Does the game provide meaningful positions for the shy or uncertain student?

Step 3: Review the surface structure.
- Are the rules easy to learn and appropriate for the age group?
- Does the surface structure (eg, constructing sets, following linear paths) support the basic purpose of the game?
- Is the game an enjoyable experience for the players?

Step 4: Determine the deep structure.
- Does the scoring system reinforce the application of academic skills?
- Does the scoring system take into account the range of difficulty in game tasks?
- Does the scoring system provide different ways to win (a non-zero-sum game)?
- Are cheating and bluffing excluded by the rules and/or reinforcement structure of the game?
- Are the moves or plays in the game essential and supportive of the academic purpose?

REFERENCES

Bell, M (1982) 'STRATAGEM: A problem-solving game for use in revision', *Simulation/Games for Learning*, **12**, 4, 157-64.

De Vries, D and Edwards, K (1973) 'Learning games and student teams: Their effects on classroom process', *American Educational Research Journal*, **10**, 307-18.

Ellington, H, Addinall, E and Percival, F (1982) 'Simulation/game design', *Simulation/Games for Learning*, **12**, 2, 74-7.

Gagné, R (1977) *The Conditions of Learning* (3rd edn), New York: Holt, Rinehart and Winston.

Gagné, R (1985) *The Conditions of Learning* (4th edn), New York: Holt, Rinehart and Winston.

Gagné, R and Briggs, L J (1979) *Principles of Instructional Design* (2nd edn), New York: Holt, Rinehart and Winston.

Gredler, M (1990) 'Analysing deep structure in games and simulations', *Simulation/Games for Learning*, **20**, 3, 329-34.

Gredler, M (1992) *Learning and Instruction* (2nd edn), New York: Macmillan.

Humphrey, J H (1970) *Teaching Slow Learners Through Active Games*, Springfield, Ill: Humphrey and Sullivan.

Jones, K (1987) 'Interactive Events, National Differences and Characterization', in Crookall, D, Klabbers, J H G, Coote, A, Saunders, D, Cecchini, A and Piane, A D (eds) *Simulation-gaming in Education and Training*, 25–32, Oxford: Pergamon Press.

Lundy, J (1985) 'The effects of competition in business games', in van Ments, M and Hearnden, K (eds) *Effective Use of Games and Simulation*, 199–208, Loughborough: SAGSET/Loughborough University of Technology.

Skinner, B (1953) *Science and Human Behaviour*, New York: Macmillan.

Skinner, B F (1984) 'Skinner's Technology of Teaching' (interview by J O Green), *Classroom Computer Learning*, **4**, 5, 23–9.

Thiagarajan, S and Stolovitch, H (1980) 'Frame games: An evaluation', in Horn, R and Cleaves, A (eds) *The Guide to Simulations/Games for Training*, 98–9, Beverly Hills, CA: Sage.

The Would-Be Gentleman, Intellimation, PO Box 1530, Santa Barbara, CA 93116-1530.

3 Computer games in the classroom

The application of computers in the development of academic games for the classroom has yet to utilize the unique potential of the technology. However, a restricted use of computer capabilities at this point should not be surprising. Any new technology, when first introduced, is used to implement already-existing practices. The automobile, for example, when first developed, was viewed as merely an efficient means for getting from the farm to town. Eventually, however, the automobile changed the fabric of daily life. Today, commuters travel daily by car from suburbs to cities to go to work and the family holiday is often a car journey.

Two major issues in the design of computer games for academic use are discussed in this chapter. They are first, the current efforts to imitate the structure of manual games and second, models of academic games that utilize the potential of the computer to store databases of information and to manage various types of data.

COMPUTER VERSIONS OF MANUAL GAME ORGANIZATION

Microcomputers differ from other devices used in manual games in a variety of ways. These differences can lead to problems in both surface and deep structure when computer games imitate manual games without careful attention to computer issues.

Types of interactions

The paraphernalia used in manual classroom games either facilitate play in the game and/or provide an ongoing visual record of the progress of the players. Markers, chips, draughts and cards, for example, are moved, traded or exchanged by players at each turn. Game boards, cards with labelled squares that may be covered with markers, or displayed sets of playing cards indicate the progress of the players during the game. Each of these artefacts, however, plays a subordinate role to the primary events in the game – that of the players' interactions with each other and with the game tasks.

In contrast, the microcomputer is not a mechanism for group interaction. First, player attention is focused on the computer screen which is the source of the action. Second, only one person at a time can interact with the technology. Therefore, if the microcomputer is the centre of the action, games that involve two or three teams of two or more players each are not practical. Four to six players cannot comfortably gather around the screen and be an integral part of the activity.

Therefore, when the computer is the delivery mechanism for a game, four competitive structures are feasible. They are 1) two players competing against each other; 2) one player or a two-person team striving to out-perform a pre-set standard; 3) one player (or a two-person team) competing against the computer which is also a player; and 4) two players competing against each other and against the computer which is also acting as a player.

In addition, when the manual game concept of completing tasks and advancing in the play is transferred to the computer, the technology becomes the delivery mechanism for all game events. That is, directions, descriptions of goals, presentation of tasks or questions and feedback to the players are delivered by the computer. Thus, it is the mechanism that both organizes the play and becomes the major source of interaction for the players.

Surface structure issues

Several aspects of game design for computers can result in impediments to the play as well as sending inappropriate messages about the technology. They are confusing directions, inappropriate graphics and poorly-designed game mechanics.

Task presentation
Several important rules should be observed in developing directions for microcomputer games. First, they should be simple with a minimum of verbiage. Second, the vocabulary level should match the age level of the players. When the manual describes a game as appropriate for several age levels, such as 6- to 11-year-olds, the directions are often above the vocabulary of the youngest group.

Third, the directions should not omit important steps. In one computer game, for example, striking the 'cap lock' key so that the computer will receive the student's initial responses to questions about viewing the list of topics, is omitted. (This step can only be found by searching the game manual.)

Fourth, at least one opportunity should be provided to practise a sample task prior to the start of the game. This prevents the player from losing points through misunderstanding the task or the rules.

Fifth, avoid multi-step directions whenever possible. If three-step directions are essential, each step should be presented one at a time accompanied by an example representative of the tasks in the game.

Developers of microcomputer exercises for the classroom, for the most part, have not been sensitive to these requirements. Many exercises include a full screen of instructions presented at one time. Once the directions have been viewed by the player, they disappear when the 'return' or 'enter' key is struck. Also, most programs do not include options during play to review the directions.

Use of graphics

Computer games make use of graphics in a variety of ways. Genies appear in caves, clowns appear and disappear and so on. Crookall *et al.* (1986, p 248) note that graphics or sound effects initially appear to enhance the exercise by making it more enjoyable or gripping. However, these features draw so much attention that other key components of the exercise often tend to be ignored.

A second problem is the inappropriate curriculum message sent to students with the use of fancy graphics that are not an integral part of the task. Skinner (1984) noted that 'jazzing up' the material to give a student false interest sends the message that the material is not worthy of being learned in its own right. Instead, success in applying the knowledge should be the focus of computer exercises.

Graphics, therefore, should only be used when they are an integral part of the exercise. However, they should not be used to create tasks that are more easily implemented in a paper and pencil format. For example, some exercises utilize a visually organized matrix for puzzle-like problems that is a complex version of noughts-and-crosses (Edens and Gredler, 1990). However, operating the computer to reveal or to insert objects or symbols in the matrices is more time-consuming and difficult than in the paper and pencil version.

One appropriate use of graphics is in the replication of a popular television quiz show, *Jeopardy*. The game board headed with different categories with sums of money in each column from $100 to $500 is the basis of the TV game. The computer version reproduces the game board in colour. The player chooses an amount, and is shown the answer associated with that amount. The player then has a limited amount of time to complete a 'what', 'where', or 'who' question that fits the displayed answer. Graphics are also used in the computer version to portray the game show moderator and the players. Although this use of graphics preserves the sequence of events in the actual quiz show, it is less effective than the portrayal of the game board.

Learner control of game mechanics

When students are playing manual games, the game does not stall if they are unable to answer a question. The player loses an opportunity to move forward or to earn points, but the game continues.

In contrast, computer games often do not provide options for students to bypass tasks that are too complex or items they are unable to answer. (The game could easily be programmed to accept 'P' for a 'Pass' to bypass a particular question and striking the 'escape' key to end the round.) Instead, the computer waits for the student to input an answer. Since the only way for the player to continue in the game is to strike a key or type in a word, players are forced to enter random answers. The result, of course, is that the computer evaluates the student input as wrong (a conclusion that is no surprise to the student). The ultimate result, however, is frustration and possibly an increase in random guessing. The curriculum messages sent by software with these problems is that the computer itself is either mysterious to operate or difficult to learn to use.

Deep structure issues

Deep structure refers to the psychological mechanisms that explain the nature of the interactions in a game or simulation. In academic games, deep structure is reflected in the skills that lead to success and the behaviours that earn reinforcement.

Nature of the academic skill

The skills implemented in microcomputer games should be capabilities that are important in the curriculum (as indicated in Table 2.1 in the previous chapter). However, three problems are noted in the types of skills found in microcomputer games. One is that the games often require only the skill of recall and none of the higher levels of cognitive skills.

An example is the game *Safari Search*. The cover describes it as a game that facilitates visual discrimination, number recognition and counting. However, the manual, which is accurate, describes the skill as that of recall. The player initially is shown a 3 × 4 matrix with different versions of a particular object (such as flowers) in each cell. The image is withdrawn and the student is required to remember which type of object belongs in which cell.

Such an exercise is a puzzle (Edens and Gredler, 1990). The goal for the player is to locate or to arrange objects in a rectangular array. The task is one in which the player either manipulates puzzle components or searches for the correct puzzle piece. Although the puzzles may be quickly solved using spatial memory, they also may be solved eventually by guessing.

A second problem in several computer games is that poor game construction reinforces guessing by the players. For example, the goal of the game may be for students to implement thinking skills, yet the game tasks are so poorly constructed that they do not differentiate guessing from deductive reasoning. An example is *The Game Show* in which the clues for the answers have not been selected to facilitate deductive reasoning. For example, the first clue for the first item in 'Animals' is 'a source of meat for many people'. This clue is too general; it does not require delimiting possible choices on the basis of two or more interlocking items of information, ie, reasoning about the answer.

Another shortcoming of such a general clue is that typically, the computer is programmed only to accept one particular answer. In the 'Animals' category of *The Game Show*, 'pig' is programmed as the correct answer to 'a source of food'. Thus, the player who answers 'chicken', 'fish', 'cattle', and so on is penalised for not guessing the *pre-programmed* answer. Such a practice in an educational setting is inappropriate.

Uses of reinforcement
Success at a game is a powerful reinforcer for the strategies used in the exercise. Skinner (1953) indicates that mastery of the environment in the form of mastering skills such as sports and those involved in crafts is also a powerful reinforcer. In other words, successfully operating a microcomputer when combined with success in academic games is a powerful contingency for strengthening academic behaviours.

The contingencies in a game should reinforce appropriate behaviours and provide no reinforcement for inappropriate or inefficient behaviours. Unfortunately, the reinforcement contingencies in many computer exercises are defective (Vargas, 1986). In other words, the student is reinforced by success regardless of the strategy that is used. That is, in a problem-solving game, there often is no pay-off for using logic (which requires work) instead of randomly selecting one alternative after another.

Another serious flaw is that some games often inadvertently *reinforce the student for making errors*. For example, in most computer exercises, the computer screen changes in some way after the student inputs a choice. The student's input alters the immediate computer environment and this often is a reinforcing event for the student.

Another difficulty arises when the consequences that follow wrong answers by the student are more interesting than the feedback for correct answers. In one computer exercise, for example, a little man jumps up and down and waves his arms after a wrong answer. Students, instead of solving the problems for the correct answers, enter a variety of incorrect solutions for the opportunity to see the little man jump up and down.

Finally, players should not be punished for wrong answers or for failing to answer correctly on the first try. For example, *The Game Show* gives each player 10 points prior to the first clue and then proceeds to subtract points for each clue that is not followed immediately by a correct answer. The play is also slowed prior to the presentation of a new set of clues for a new object while the computer calculates and displays the number of points remaining to the player. Instead of this procedure, the players should earn points for correct answers and the player who uses the least number of clues should earn the higheset score. For example, players may earn as many as ten points for using only one or two clues; nine points for three; seven points for four clues; and so on. Also, points should be displayed only at the end of a round (four or five objects/events).

Flaws in the nature of the task established for the game and the behaviours that generate success create exercises that are inappropriate for classroom use. Further, the danger is that students, from such an experience, may reject the computer as an aid to both thinking and learning.

MODELS OF COMPUTER GAMES

An important issue in the development of computer games is the extent of computer or learner control over the events in the game. The three levels are total computer control, shared control between the computer and the learner, and learner control. Consideration of these levels also identifies different paradigms for constructing computer-delivered games.

Computer-controlled games

A typical game paradigm is that of the player receiving a question, responding to the question and then receiving information as to the correctness of the answer. If the answer is wrong, the next player or team takes a turn. If the answer is correct, the player (or team) advances in the game.

This basic decision sequence is the model currently implemented in the majority of computer games. In this model, the evaluative and branching capabilities of the computer are used only in a primitive way. That is, only a simple correct/not correct evaluation of the student's response is made.

Some computer games permit the student to choose both the topic and difficulty level of the questions in the exercise. This procedure provides some variation in the content of the questions that will appear in the game. However, the basic decision structure of the game does not change.

This model is appropriate for some uses, however. Teachers indicate that games constructed for basic skills, such as addition and subtraction, are useful for students who are having difficulty with those skills. That is, the student can play a game which permits him or her to practise the skills without being embarrassed in front of the other students. Since the student is typically playing to achieve a particular pre-set standard, the game assesses the student's level of mastery. The computer also provides a print-out of the player's errors in the game for the teacher.

This model is not limited to only recall and basic skills. Questions may be developed to test students' understanding of concepts and rules. Also, the computer can be programmed to adjust the difficulty level of questions up or down, depending on the player's pattern of correct answers or errors.

Shared control of game events

A game in which both the learner and the computer share control over game events is not one in which the computer repeatedly presents questions or tasks for which the player selects or generates an answer. Instead, shared control implies that the learner has choices as to the variables to be addressed and the way in which these variables will be manipulated.

One paradigm for shared control of game events is a data-management game. The computer proposes a finite set of variables and allocates resources to the player. Then the player or team, applying a knowledge base, assigns resources to one or more of the variables in a succession of decision periods. The computer continually tabulates the player's resources as they wax and wane, providing an update at each decision period. Points are added or subtracted to the player's score according to the logic and appropriateness of the player's decisions. A stock market game in which the player earns points for investments in under-rated stocks is an example.

An example of a data-management game that provides a measure of player control is *The Would-Be Gentleman* created by Carolyn Lougee (1988). The game is appropriate for advanced secondary school and college students. Set in 17th century France, the game takes the player (or team) through two decision points each year (autumn and spring) from September 1638 until September 1715. The goal is to maximize the prestige of the Marin family over two generations and to acquire the highest possible social standing in 1715.

The decisions to be made and the changes in the player's social prestige score reflect the economic realities of the 17th century. Investment decisions include buying or selling land, venal offices, textile shares, leases and *rentes* (annuities). Management decisions include the rental of land owned by the family and the sales of grain that accrue to the landowner from share-cropping or leasing the land. Success in the game, ie, maximizing social prestige points, requires a knowledge of the France of Louis XIV, the Sun King. That is, wealth alone does not lead to social status.

The game is designed for the Macintosh computer and player decisions are entered using a mouse. The computer provides an ongoing account of the player's standing in the game. A box in the lower right corner of the screen shows the season and year (eg, autumn 1690), the age of the head of the family, prestige points earned to date, total wealth and cash. This record is updated after each player decision.

49

Although the author refers to the exercise as a simulation (very likely because of the historical accuracy of many of the consequences), she notes that the exercise 'creates a fiction: the open-ended decision-making combines historically-valid fragments into wholly novel behavior' (Lougee, 1988, p 11). Also, the game attaches points to social prestige in a manner that is solely for the convenience of the game. That is, in 17th century France or any other social setting, social prestige does not translate into a specified number of points. Thus, the exercise is an academic game that makes use of the player's knowledge and understanding of a particular historical period.

The game also makes use of the data storage and evaluative capabilities of the computer. After each play, the computer compares the player's decision with a pre-determined mathematical model and adjusts the score accordingly.

Another paradigm for shared control is the discovery learning paradigm. That is, the student (or team) chooses the subject area and the topic. The computer then presents a brief 2-3 sentence scenario to the player. The goal is to determine the person or major event that is a key element in the scenario. The scenarios may be developed in a variety of subject areas, such as history, literature, social studies, psychology, science and others.

The student may ask the computer a series of yes/no questions in order to determine the person or major event. In other words, the game is a sophisticated version of *Twenty Questions*. The player, in order to earn maximum points, must implement an efficient questioning strategy that eliminates as many answers as possible with one question.

Because such games emphasize the use of logical strategies, they are appropriate for two players responding as a team. Discussions of strategy are likely to be seen by the players as advantageous in winning the game. Therefore, the interaction is not restricted to player and computer.

Learner-controlled games

In a learner-controlled game, several answers to the proposed situations may be correct. The player (or team) receives points for an accurate fit between his or her answers, and the logic of the reasons the player proposes for the soundness of the answer. For example, the computer may present a brief 3-4 sentence scenario. The player then describes in 1-3 sentences the person or key event that fits the scenario. Reasons for the selection are also entered into the computer by the player(s). The computer evaluates the choice as either fitting the parameters of the stated situation or not and then evaluates the logic of the reasons provided by the student. Any answer that is logically consistent with the scenario earns points.

Like the *Twenty Questions* exercise, scenarios may be developed in any of several subject areas. Also, these problems are appropriate for two players interacting as a team.

However, in the *Twenty Questions* exercise the player has control only over the strategy that is used to determine the one pre-selected answer. In the learner-controlled exercise, the only requirement is the logic of the answer.

Such games, while theoretically possible, are difficult to design. Also, extensive trials are required in order that possible answers that did not occur to the developers, but which are correct, are included.

Discussion

Computer games that are computer controlled in terms of the specific events that the players engage in can be developed to require the academic skills referred to by Gagné as intellectual skills (recall Table 2.1 in Chapter 2). However, computer games that allow participants to execute different strategies and/or to develop different answers require a different type of mental skill. Success in the game requires that the learner direct and manage his or her thinking in an efficient and effective manner. Variables must be noted, consequences of actions must be thought about in advance and then a course of action must be developed. These mental abilities are of the type referred to by Gagné (1977; 1985) as *cognitive strategies*. Specifically, they are the capabilities of managing one's thinking and learning in an efficient and effective manner.

Thus, unlike manual games, the computer has the capability to deliver games that require the application of cognitive strategies. Manual games, which lack the computational and rapid data-retrieval and evaluation capability of the computer, are, for the most part, limited to verbal information and intellectual skills.

EVALUATING COMPUTER GAMES FOR THE CLASSROOM

Step 1: Identify the type of game.
- Is the game computer-controlled, shared control or learner-controlled?
- If shared control, does the game involve data-management or guided discovery?
- If computer-controlled, which academic skills are required for success?

Step 2: Analyse the deep structure of the game.
- Does the game allow success through random guessing?
- Is the player punished for correct answers that were not programmed into the exercise?

- Is reinforcement provided for correct answers only when players use appropriate strategies?
- Is reinforcement avoided for incorrect answers and/or inappropriate strategies?
- Does the game avoid subtracting points for wrong answers or poor strategies?

Step 3: Review the surface structure of the game.
- Are the directions complete, simple, clear and easy to execute?
- Is the vocabulary at the appropriate level for the designated age group?
- Are graphics implemented only as a functional game component?
- Does the game use graphics to create a game that is more easily executed in a paper-and-pencil format?
- Does the game provide mechanisms so that the player does not get stalled during play?

REFERENCES

Crookall, D, Martin, A, Saunders, D and Coote, A (1986) 'Human and computer involvement in simulation', *Simulation and Games*, **17**, 3, 345–75.

Edens, K and Gredler, M (1990) 'A further analysis of computer-based simulations', *Simulations/Games for Learning*, **19**, 2, 76–81.

Gagné, R (1977) *The Conditions of Learning*, (3rd edn), New York: Holt, Rinehart & Winston.

Gagné, R (1985) *The Conditions of Learning*, (4th edn), New York: Holt, Rinehart & Winston.

Lougee, C (1988) 'The Would-be Gentleman: A historical simulation of the France of Louis XIV', *History Microcomputer Review*, **4**, 1, 7–14.

Skinner, B F (1953) *Science and Human Behaviour*, New York: Macmillan.

Skinner, B F (1984) In J O Green, Skinner's 'technology of teaching', *Classroom Computer Learning*, **4**, 5, 23–9.

Vargas, J (1986) 'Instructional Design Flaws in Computer-assisted Instruction', *Phi Delta Kappan*, **64**, 738–44.

4 Characteristics of tactical-decision simulations

The task for participants in social-process simulations is to interact with each other in their efforts to achieve a particular social or political goal or to address a particular challenge. In contrast, the task in tactical-decision simulations is to interact with a complex evolving problem or crisis and bring it to a safe and/or logical conclusion. The differences in these two orientations establish different design parameters for the two types of simulations.

PRE-DESIGN ISSUES

The three types of tactical-decision simulations are diagnostic, crisis-management and data-management exercises. Issues common to all three types are the general purpose, the nature of the problem or task, the relationships of identified roles to the problem and control of events.

General purpose

An important characteristic of tactical-decision simulations is that they require the application of particular types of problem-solving skills. They are the capabilities to:

> select, process, and interpret data; use a variety of resources; order priorities of data seeking and decision making; take appropriate action; manipulate the situation to alter it; monitor the effects of these manipulations, and readjust decisions or actions to respond to changing conditions (McGuire et al., 1975, p 7).

These skills are among those referred to by Gagné (1977; 1985) as *cognitive strategies*. Specifically, these capabilities are the skills involved in managing one's own learning, remembering and thinking. Organizing information to analyse one's financial status or selecting the appropriate information to diagnose the causes of a problem are examples. Other terms applied to these skills or capabilities are *strategic knowledge* (Greeno, 1978), *self-management behaviours* (Skinner, 1968; 1987) and *metacognition* (Anderson, 1990).

Capabilities in addressing problems are important in every walk of life. Often, however, practice in problem-solving involves textbook problems followed by some type of clinic, practicum or field experience. One deficiency in such a practice is the lack of opportunity to develop one's cognitive strategies in a systematic way. The student may make errors in the field that could have been corrected earlier.

Another problem is the difficulty in accurately assessing a student's specific strengths and weaknesses in problem-solving in an internship. Often in the clinic experience or internship, the situations to which different students are exposed vary in complexity and difficulty. Thus, any profile of student strengths and weaknesses developed in such a situation is dependent, in large measure, on the cases the student receives.

The use of tactical-decision simulations can alleviate these problems. Business schools and colleges have implemented data-management simulations since the late 1950s and these simulations are also appropriate for other curriculum areas. Medical schools in the United States have used diagnostic simulations both as learning experiences and assessment tools since the early 1970s.

However, tactical-decision simulations are not limited to curricula that teach students to solve problems they will face in their future careers. Instead, they are useful in any curriculum area in which problem-solving is important. One precursor of data-management simulations, for instance, is *The Sumerian Game*. Developed in the 1960s, the exercise provided experience in managing the country's grain supply for the benefit of the citizens and the economic status of the country.

Nature of the problem, crisis or task

A tactical-decision simulation establishes a situation in which participants make 'a number of interdependent decisions in a dynamic environment in which uncertainty exists and in which no direct analytical solution to the overall problem exists' (Greenlaw and Frey, 1967, p 4). Thus, the problem addressed by the participant(s) should not be a textbook statement of characteristics, such that the individuals can solve the problem in a few minutes. Furthermore, the exercise cannot be a case study in which the details of a problem or crisis are described and the individual selects or determines a correct answer.

Sometimes, in efforts to develop a complex task, designers introduce complication after complication. The result is control of the exercise by random events, which is not desirable, or too many variables for the participants to manage.

The task should be one that requires sequential decision-making. In diagnostic and crisis-management simulations, participants initiate enquiries to determine the exact nature and scope of the problem or crisis, interpret the data and implement strategies to resolve the situation. In data-management simulations, in contrast, the participants are manipulating variables over a period of time in an effort to improve the status of an institution, country or individual. The variables typically are financial or economic.

Finally, the problem and the variables included in the simulation must be credible and meaningful to the participants. For example, establishing a data-management simulation in which secondary school pupils take the role of the head of the family and budget the family's resources is meaningful. In contrast, managing the financial resources of a province or state may be treated as a game.

Relationship of identified roles to the problem

Three issues are inherent in the relationship of participant roles to the simulation. One issue, already mentioned, is that the problem or crisis must be one that the participants in their roles feel compelled to address.

Second, the role assigned to the participant is one that allows maximum opportunity to exercise initiatives, select relevant data and/ or implement any of a variety of strategies. Bank executives, for instance, determine the goals for their institution, identify the data that will provide them with the information they require and determine the ways in which variables are to be manipulated (data-management simulation).

Third, the participant is empowered with the authority and the responsibility to resolve the particular problem or crisis and this empowerment is known to the participants. For example, students in archaeology classes may take roles as members of a team in the field in order to deduce the nature of an ancient civilisation from an archaeological dig (diagnostic simulation). The roles are determined by the needed types of data analysis, such as lithics expert, tool expert and so on. The team members are expected to conclude their investigations with a report to which each 'expert' contributes a section.

Control of events

An important requirement for any tactical-decision simulation is that the exercise should not be dominated by random events. In one group of so-called computer simulations, discussed in Chapter 7, the outcomes are completely controlled by a series of chance events. Referred to as *variable-assignment exercises* (Gredler, 1986), these exercises convey the message that hard work and intelligent decision-making do not influence life outcomes. Thus, an important factor in reality of function for participants is that their decisions and actions are major determinants of the consequences that they experience in the simulation.

Therefore, when the framework for the exercise is developed, only one or two plausible complications may be selected that are not consequences of participant actions. Otherwise, all changes or effects on the problem are the result of participant decision-making.

In other words, a major characteristic of tactical-decision simulations is that participants are in control of the sequence of events. They select data they believe to be relevant and interpret and manipulate the data in their efforts to achieve the goal of the exercise.

In summary, several parameters are important in developing credible tactical-decision simulations. They are the nature of the particular problem or task, the relationship of the participant's role to the problem, and the control of events throughout the simulation. Careful attention to each of these factors contributes to reality of function for the participants in the simulation.

ESTABLISHING THE FRAMEWORK

In social-process simulations, participants set about addressing particular social goals or priorities that are indicated by the roles they have taken. Examples include supporting or working to defeat the building of a new bridge that threatens the nesting grounds of a rare bird, attempting to become assimilated into a strange culture and others.

Tactical-decision simulations, in contrast, revolve around data interpretation and management. In other words, the interactions that propel tactical-decision simulations are between the participants and a complex problem, crisis or task. Participants face an uncertain situation in which they must select or manipulate relevant data, receive updated information and interpret the new information. Examples include determining the causes of an air accident, managing the finances of one's 'family' for a year, and discovering the source of contaminated antibiotics suspected in a hospital death.

Although tactical-decision simulations are often team exercises, interaction among participants is secondary to the data-collection and interpretation activities. Therefore, designers cannot simply establish an issue and roles with different perspectives on the issue. Instead, the simulation must be designed so that success requires the systematic and rational interpretation of data by the participants. Two important steps in the design process are developing a blueprint and selecting the format for the simulation.

Developing a blueprint

Both diagnostic and crisis-management simulations are complex problem-solving exercises that require both data interpretation and specific strategies to resolve the problem or crisis. After the problem and roles are selected, developers should prepare a general sequence of likely events. It should include the types of information that participants are likely to request and when, the information to be provided in response to each request, types of management steps that participants may initiate and changes in the problem resulting from those actions. In other words, a blueprint that indicates possible requests and actions of the participants and related responses to participant decisions is the basis for developing specific materials for the simulation. Because one purpose of the simulation is to allow both weak and strong students to find plausible courses of action, a comprehensive array of possible actions should be included. For example, when attempting to arrive at the diagnosis of a patient's illness, the 'doctor' who is uncertain about the implications of the symptoms is likely to request several different tests, some of which may seem plausible but which do not contribute to the diagnosis.

Data-management simulations, in contrast, require participants to manipulate variables and/or to allocate resources in an effort to improve the status of an individual, a group, a business or an institution. An important planning step for these simulations is the identification of key variables and the relationships to other economic or financial variables. Several factors important in developing a comprehensive mathematical model of the relationships among variables are discussed in Chapter 7.

Format

The development of a general sequence of simulation events is influenced in part by the format selected for the exercise. That is, the simulation may be either a closed-structure or an open-structure exercise. A closed-structure simulation is a pre-packaged exercise. One early data-management exercise designed to acquaint the participant with general business and economic principles is *FINANSIM* (Greenlaw and Frey, 1967). The individual completes a set of decision sheets in each financial period that are then analysed by computer according to a pre-determined mathematical model. The completed analysis and any reported changes in variables not under the participant's control are used by the individual in making the next set of decisions.

Diagnostic simulations in the closed-structure format developed in the 1960s and early 1970s were produced in booklet form. The answers to requests for information and the consequences of participant actions on the problem were reproduced in printed latent images. The participant discovered the information related to his or her choices by using a special pen. In the 1970s, computer-delivered exercises replaced the booklet format. Currently, closed-structure simulations are beginning to be developed using videodisc technology. With this computer-controlled technology, the individual can view images of actual scenes, objects and events. An advantage of the technology over the computer-delivered exercise is that participants can see and hear responses to their enquiries and also observe the physical effects of actions they have taken.

The closed-structure diagnostic simulation is a multiple-branching exercise in which the participant can pursue any of a variety of courses of action. The participant chooses among data-gathering and data-management categories and then chooses from among the available options in the selected category. Information is provided to the participant on his or her requests, another category is selected and the exercise continues.

Although the possible options are pre-determined by the designer in diagnostic simulations, the exercises are not necessarily superficial experiences. If the sets of options and their related information are well designed, the exercise can be one that meets the criteria for reality of function for tactical-decision simulation. That is, the participant accepts the responsibility of solving a problem appropriate to the associated role and becomes mentally engaged with the situation.

Closed-structure simulations are appropriate for situations in which an individual in a particular role solves a complex problem. They are used extensively in medical schools and also in programmes for other health-care workers and psychologists. One advantage of this format is that it provides a record of student selection so that the student's approaches to the problem and deductions may be analysed later by the instructor. Thus, these simulations are appropriate for a variety of curriculum areas. Strategies for developing closed-structure simulations that contribute to reality of function are discussed in Chapter 5.

Closed-structure simulations are not appropriate for team exercises. The format does not allow for the direct interaction of each role with the particular problem. Instead, some members of the team, by default, become spectators. However, problems or tasks faced by teams are not solved by team members waiting for one of the group to receive information about requested data or prior actions taken by participants.

Open-structure simulations are appropriate when the discovery of essential data is an integral component of the problem-solving process and/or the situation requires a team approach. Some police training programmes, for example, place recruits in simulated road accidents in which he or she must determine the events that led up to the accident (McKelvie, 1978). Other examples of open-structure simulations are a crisis-management team attempting to deploy resources following a natural disaster, and a management team attempting to improve the profitability of a bank.

Participants in open-structure simulations take specific roles with particular responsibilities. Initial stimuli to which they respond are the content of the problem, the background information and the setting. As participants assimilate this information, they initiate requests for additional data (diagnostic and crisis-management simulations) or they establish goals and allocate resources to variables (data-management simulations).

The purpose of the team exercise is for relevant decision-makers to work together to resolve a situation. Therefore, although the participants do interact with each other, the primary interactions are between the participants and the problem. In other words, tactical-decision simulations are not simply group discussions of a multifaceted problem that involves requesting or manipulating data.

Instead, a well-designed simulation structures the situation so that participants focus on their role in relation to the problem. In addition to the prepared sources of information that participants may request, the flow of events may be maintained in a variety of ways. One is that officials or others with a legitimate interest in the investigation in diagnostic or crisis-management simulations may request information or reports from the participants. In data-management simulations, weekly, monthly or quarterly reports reflect changes in variables and/or economic conditions. Also, peripheral roles taken by members of the project staff provide a mechanism for interjecting new events and/or information into the situation. Specific examples are discussed in Chapters 5 and 6.

In summary, simulations consist of four major components. They are the a) assigned roles; b) opening scene and/or background information; c) stimuli to which participants respond; and d) reactions to participant actions. The design of tactical-decision simulations requires careful attention to the stimuli that precipitate participant actions and the reactions or responses to their decisions. Development of a rich database for participants, which allows them to pursue any of several lines of inquiry, can establish a climate in which reality of function for various problem-solving roles is established.

REFERENCES

Anderson, J R (1990) *Cognitive Psychology and its Implications*, (3rd edn), New York: Freeman.

Gagné, R M (1977) *The Conditions of Learning*, (3rd edn), New York: Holt, Rinehart & Winston.

Gagné, R M (1985) *The Conditions of Learning*, (4th edn), New York: Holt, Rinehart & Winston.

Gredler, M (1986) 'A taxonomy of microcomputer simulations', *Educational Technology*, **26**, 3, 7–12.

Greenlaw, P and Frey, M (1967) *FINANSIM: A Finance Management Simulation*, Scranton, PA: International Textbook Company.

Greeno, J G (1978) 'Nature of problem-solving abilities', in Estes, W (ed.) *Handbook of Learning and Cognitive Processes*, 239–70, Hillsdale, NJ: Erlbaum.

McGuire, C, Solomon, L and Bashook, P (1975) *Construction and Use of Written Simulations*, Houston, TX: The Psychological Corporation.

McKelvie, J (1978) 'Simulation in police training', *SAGSET*, **8**, 1, 15–19.

Skinner, B F (1968) *The Technology of Teaching*, New York: Appleton-Century-Crofts.

Skinner, B F (1987) *Upon Further Reflection*, Englewood Cliffs, NJ: Prentice-Hall.

5 Diagnostic simulations

Solving complex evolving problems is a facet of various walks of life. School personnel analyse pupil actions and other factors in order to develop effective ways of managing discipline problems and archaeologists seek to piece together past civilisations from fragments of artefacts and writings.

Diagnostic simulations provide such experiences. Taking roles as medical doctors, teachers, psychologists, archaeologists and others, participants begin with sketchy information about an event relevant to their assigned roles. The information may be a patient's symptoms, a pupil's behaviour, or several layers of soil imbedded with fragments of artefacts and bones. Participants then seek additional data to help them determine the nature of the situation and implement a strategy for diagnosing the patient or client, reconstructing an ancient civilisation and so on.

OVERVIEW

Diagnostic simulations are the descendents of the early in-tray exercises. They differ both in the extent of problems addressed and their role and purpose in learning.

Early developments

The first in-tray exercises were developed in the 1950s. One such exercise is *Jefferson Township* developed in 1959 by school personnel. Centered on a 'typical' school system, the simulation included roles for any of several administrators, including school superintendent, elementary principal, high school principal and business director (Wynn, 1964).

Introductory materials were composed of written documents (personnel records, achievement test results and annotated school policies), films on the community and school and tape-recordings of excerpts of meetings and parent-conferences (Wynn, 1964, p 171). Although comprehensive these materials required about five hours of the participant's time.

The exercise presented a series of written communications to which the participant responded in writing. Examples are a note reporting a broken window that the parents refuse to pay for, data on a pupil having difficulty in class, a letter from a parent complaining about a teacher's letter to the editor of the local newspaper and so on. The participants' written responses to each of these problems formed the basis for later group discussion.

Later in-tray exercises provided feedback to participants on their actions in the form of changes in the problem and the reactions of others. This feedback was also written and might include memos from others, telephone messages and so on.

In-tray exercises are composed of discrete specific events. In contrast, diagnostic simulations are complex problems that require definition, analysis and management by the participants. Medical schools initiated the use of diagnostic simulations in the training of physicians. Much of the early work on problem development, structure and design was done by Christine McGuire and her colleagues at the University of Illinois College of Medicine (see McGuire *et al.*, 1975).

As indicated in Chapter 4, the first diagnostic simulations were developed in booklet form with multiple branches. Beginning in the late 1970s, the use of booklets was, for the most part, discontinued and replaced by computer-delivered simulations. Well-designed diagnostic simulations have been developed in the health sciences (see Jones and Keith, 1983; Bidwell *et al.*, 1985; Pickell *et al.*, 1986) school psychology (eg, de Mesquita, 1987) and other fields.

Uses

The most extensive use is in the clinical areas of the health sciences. However, diagnostic simulations can be used effectively in other curriculum areas. For instance, a major reason for the development of several air accident investigations was that students failed to exercise a careful methodological approach at their first accident site (Rolfe and Taylor, 1984). When actually faced with the equivalent of finding the needle in the haystack, students picked up items before photographing the site, tramped on ground marks or simply ventured random guesses about the cause (p 150).

Moreover, Willems and his co-workers found that students in law, social geography, science and sociology were often unable to apply knowledge they had acquired to the task of solving problems (Willems, 1981). As indicated in Chapter 4, diagnostic simulations can assist in overcoming weaknesses in students' problem-solving capabilities.

Major characteristics

Diagnostic simulations are appropriate for problems or situations that require sequential decision-making. Depending on the type of problem, the simulation may require the discovery, evaluation and interpretation of relevant data (eg, archaeological investigation) or the selection, interpretation and management of relevant data (eg, diagnosing and managing a client's problems).

The interrelated decision-making creates a situation in which the outcome is influenced by prior decisions of the participant (McGuire, *et al.*, 1975). Thus, the complications that occur differ from participant to participant depending on the particular procedure selected early in the exercise (p 9). If the participant fails to enquire about certain relevant types of information, resolving the problem or preventing a critical turn of events will be more difficult and problematic.

Consider the situation in which the participant in his or her role as a social studies teacher must deal with two high school pupils who compete with each other for the attention of their peers. Their bids for attention are disrupting the class. The teacher first must define the nature of the problem. That is, are the pupils the sole source of the problem or are other factors, such as the pace of lessons in the class or the dry nature of the particular unit of instruction, associated 'causes'? Analysis of the nature of the problem will influence the types of data selected for review, which, in turn, may prevent or add to subsequent problems in the exercise.

A second major characteristic is that the problems are not uni-dimensional. In one simulation in which participants take the roles of members of an air accident investigation team, the primary cause of the air crash is complicated by the presence of contributing factors. Some of these factors are mechanical and some are human and operational (Rolfe and Taylor, 1984, p 142).

A third characteristic of diagnostic simulations is that the exercise includes information that is plausible, but is not relevant to the optimal solution of the problem. Thus, the exercise is constructed so that participants who are unsure of the appropriate strategy to use can find options that are appealing to them.

Sub-types
Included in diagnostic simulations are two sub-types. They are client-management and 'Solve the mystery' simulations. In the client-management simulations, the participant takes the role of a profes-sional such as a teacher, a psychologist or a doctor and diagnoses and manages the problem of a student, a patient, a welfare mother or some other individual.

The mystery-resolution simulation poses a situation that is an enigma requiring detection and the management of events in order to arrive at a solution. An example is the simulation *In the Hot Seat*, in which an air accident team attempts to determine the causes of a plane crash. Other examples are those used in police training in which recruits investigate simulated road accidents (McKelvie, 1978).

This sub-type has applications to a variety of subject areas including science, literature, history and others. For example, students in an introductory archaeology course work on a constructed 'dig' in which they apply field methods to determine the nature and characteristics of a past civilization. The students, assigned particular roles on an archaeological investigating team, sift out the soil and isolate animal bone fragments and teeth, tool fragments and other artefacts. Each team member conducts tests on the materials for which he or she is responsible and analyses and writes up their findings. Thus, the participants complete the same tasks as professionals from the beginning (excavating) to the conclusion (data analysis and reporting).

Most diagnostic simulations are single-participant exercises. However, some, like the archaeology exercise, are designed for teams. The additional responsibility in these exercises is that of coordinating team members' efforts as they pursue their separate roles.

Simulations that require a team approach are developed in the open structure format as described in Chapter 4. However, diagnostic simulations intended for one role, such as school counsellor, teacher, nurse or doctor typically are developed as closed-structure exercises.

MAJOR DESIGN ISSUES

Several design issues are important in developing diagnostic simulations. They are developing the simulation framework, setting the stage, developing the events that precipitate participant actions, determining the reactions to participant decisions and exiting from the simulation. These issues are addressed somewhat differently for closed-structure and open-structure simulations.

Closed-structure simulations

Unlike the open-structure format, closed-structure simulations are pre-packaged exercises. All information, options for data interpretation and management and reactions to participant decisions are developed in advance and organized into a multiple branching exercise.

Developing the framework
The first step is to select the problem and to identify the participant's role. As indicated in Chapter 4, the problem should be one with, at most, one or two complications. Efforts to encompass a range of thinking about an area in an extensive problem that samples several aspects of a field are to be avoided (McGuire *et al.*, 1975, p 93). The participant's role is that of a problem-solver empowered to address the situation posed in the simulation. Examples include emergency department doctor, teacher, social worker and nurse.

Prior to developing the simulation components, however, a general framework is needed. McGuire *et al.*, (1975) suggest that designers

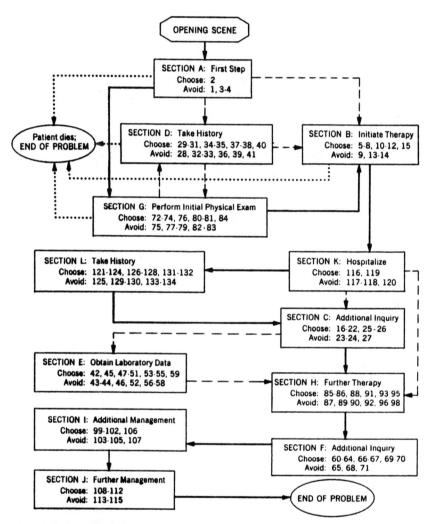

Figure 5.1 *Map of a simulation to diagnose and manage patient S L (reprinted with permission of The Psychological Corporation)*

should write a general script of the exercise. Then they should design a map of the simulation. The map indicates the opening scene, possible routes through the exercise, the major sections and any points at which an irreversible choice may be selected by a participant that will terminate the exercise.

Figure 5.1 illustrates both the major sections and associated options in a completed simulation in which the doctor is responsible for the diagnosis and management of a patient. Solid arrows indicate the optimal route through the exercise; dashed arrows indicate an alternative path in which a solution is still possible. Dotted arrows, however, indicate the path to an unsatisfactory termination of the exercise.

The map of the sections serves as a guide for developing the sets of options. However, it is not cast in concrete. Changes may be made as development proceeds.

In working through the simulation, the participant selects a particular category of data gathering or data management after the opening scene. The participant then selects several options from the set of choices in that category. Feedback on the chosen options is then presented, the student interprets the information and makes a subsequent choice of a category. This process continues until the participant resolves the situation or is exited for a fatal error.

Opening scene
The opening scene sets the stage for the simulation. It is an important component in placing the participant mentally into the situation. The opening scene should be brief and should describe the situation to be addressed in concrete yet neutral terms. It should also describe the role of the participant and precipitate the search for clues to provide definitive information as to the nature of the problem.

Essential information to be included in the opening scene are the physical setting of the problem, the participant's role and task and any limitations in terms of time, facilities or assistance available to the participant (McGuire *et al.*, 1975, p 100). In addition, since real-world problems are usually obscured by 'noise', some extraneous information should be included.

The opening scene may be presented in any of several formats, from videotape or photographs to audio-recordings. Combinations of these formats may also be used. For example, some police departments introduce simulations with a brief videotape of a crime in progress and the action is stopped when the 'police officers' enter the scene. Regardless of the selected format, the five key items of information named in the previous paragraph must be included in some way.

Options
An important factor in providing reality of function in the closed-structure format is the sets of options in the data gathering and

management phases. An essential characteristic is that the options represent both positive and negative selections. That is, the options are essential, facilitative, neutral, impeding (but not serious) and harmful.

Table 5.1 illustrates a set of five options in a simulation in which the participant is a consultant hired by the city council to determine the feasibility of desktop computers for department heads (Gallini and Gredler, 1989). The result of choosing Option 1 is that one council member is angered at being singled out and releases an inflammatory story to the local newspaper. Subsequent steps provided in the simulation following the news release allow the consultant to recover or to cause further problems by his or her actions.

Overall, the simulation should offer a balanced mix of the five option types so that the ill-informed student cannot benefit from randomly selecting options (McGuire *et al.*, 1975, p 113). Both the impeding and harmful (essential to avoid) options should represent plausible misconceptions about approaching and managing the problem.

Also important is that opportunities to act on these misconceptions must be available in all sections of the exercise (McGuire *et al.*, p 117). This practice provides the opportunity for students to pursue an inappropriate course of action to its logical conclusion and it also prevents the optimal course of action from appearing obvious. To prevent unintended cueing, each option should state a single idea in a neutral way.

Reactions to options
All reactions to available options are descriptive, not evaluative. A

Table 5.1 *Examples of a set of participant options**

OPTION	RELATIONSHIP TO THE PROBLEM
1. Interview two council members who are uncertain about supporting the use of computers	Impeding
2. Meet the city manager to request interviews of department heads	Essential
3. Ask the council secretary for a copy of original computer proposal	Neutral
4. Review minutes of city council meetings	Neutral
5. Visit some of the department heads' secretaries	Harmful

*Summarized from Gallini and Gredler (1989)

request for a blood pressure reading, for example, would report simply 'blood pressure is 140/90'. Similarly, an X-ray report would state the radiologist's objective observations, but would not include the phrase 'within normal limits'.

A particular problem in closed-structure simulations is that a continuous sequence of dry, printed statements seriously threatens reality of function for the participant. One of the advantages of videodisc technology is that it avoids this problem.

One suggestion for computer-delivered simulations is to provide meaningful formats for data presentation whenever possible. For example, a response to a request for information from a pupil's cumulative school record should reproduce pages from the record. Also, reactions from consultants and others who may be contacted for information during the simulation should be presented in the language and style of the particular individual. A classmate of a pupil with a problem, for example, will respond in a different manner than will the teacher to the school psychologist.

Finally, responses to requests for data should respect the logistical parameters involved in obtaining the information. Laboratory tests, for example, may require from 24 to 48 hours. Therefore, a time lapse should be built into the exercise consistent with other events until the results are reported. That is, the exercise should report when the results will be available and a later option for the participant should state, 'check the patient's record for new information'. However, the later option should not state 'check the patient's record for lab test X'. This wording may lead the participant who did not order the test to believe it is necessary and therefore change his or her course of action.

After the opening scene, options for all sections and the associated results are prepared and bridging segments that allow participants to move between the sections of the exercise are written. Then the simulation is implemented to ensure that participants cannot get caught in an endless loop between sections. That is, each major section of the exercise has an entry and an exit for the participant. Then the simulation is ready for trial to determine conceptual and other difficulties that may require adjustment.

Exiting from the simulation
In the closed-structure simulation, the participant continues through data gathering and problem management to the logical conclusion unless he or she makes an irretrievable 'fatal error'. Should this happen, the participant is exited immediately from the simulation.

Although the simulation is designed so that participants can recover from minor errors, an irretrievable error leads to disaster. The student is informed of the effects of the fatal error and directed to exit. Figure 5.2 illustrates this situation in the evaluation consultant simulation (Gallini and Gredler, 1989).

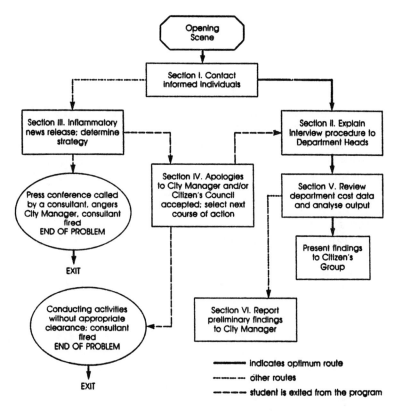

Figure 5.2 *Routes through early stages of evaluation consultant simulation (reprinted by permission of HarperCollins Publishers).*

Role of technology

The development of CD-ROM technology and videodiscs provide new opportunities for the development of closed-structure diagnostic simulations. Unlike videotape, the computer-managed videodisc is randomly accessible. Also, up to 54 000 pictures or frames can be recorded on a 30-minute videodisc. When played in real time, the viewer observes a live-action video image.

Harvard Law School, for example, has developed a series of interactive videodisc exercises in its Interactive Video Project (Miller, 1990). The project makes use of a two-screen delivery system – video and computer – designed to keep user costs at a reasonable level. The user is presented with a list of options on the computer screen, makes a selection and then views the outcome on the videoscreen. For example, in the 'Search and Seizure' lesson, the user must act to obtain a valid warrant. If he or she does not respond at key points, the warrant will be defective and the search will result in exclusion of important evidence at the trial (p 80). Although expensive, an advantage of the technology is that it can portray visually the effects of one's actions on a situation.

Reality of function

In closed-structure simulations, the scope of the problem, the possible courses of action and the results are key elements in establishing a climate of reality of function for the participants. One of the more serious errors in the closed-structure simulation is that of minimal linear branching from a restricted set of options. In addition, the reactions to participant enquiries and strategies must be both logically consistent and credible.

An example of these problems is the computer exercise *Transactions* which is intended for classroom teachers. First, a simple problem that requires only a single-step solution is presented. Specifically, the problem is that a high school pupil is continually falling asleep in the teacher's class. (The obvious solution is to ask the pupil at the end of class why he continues to fall asleep.)

The exercise provides five options, some of which lead to a two-step branch. Others lead to another set of options, *of which four are the same as the original set*. Thus, the second problem is that the exercise is 'solved' in less than three steps, even when only random guessing is used.

Third, the 'correct' decisions were determined by the designers according to the transactional analysis model. This model, intended for use in counselling and related fields, specifies that one should respond in terms of the position and thoughts of others on issues. However, the application of such a model to a situation in which a teacher has been assigned legal responsibility for a class is questionable. In summary, the exercise does not meet essential design requirements and therefore cannot provide reality of function for participants.

Open-structure simulations

The open-structure format is appropriate when the goal includes data discovery (in addition to interpretation and analysis) or the exercise requires a team approach. Two examples of team exercises are the use of archaeological 'sites' for excavation and study (Rice, 1985) and the crash investigation simulation described by Rolfe and Taylor (1984).

The open-structure simulation is an open-ended exercise in which participants can take any of several different directions. Therefore, developers of team simulations face a particular issue: they must design a situation that maintains participant interaction with the problem so that the exercise does not become a general discussion session or cease to be a problem-solving exercise.

Developing the framework

The writing of a simulation typically does not proceed in lock-step fashion in which certain steps are completed in a stated order. Instead, developers usually establish a general framework, begin designing the particular components and then work back and forth between the general framework and the specifics, altering each as is necessary.

The general parameters for an open-structure simulation consist of the problem, the team roles, the setting for the simulation and a general sequence of expected events. Problems for team exercises are often drawn from the experience of instructors or supervisors in a field setting who have identified typical errors made by students in understanding applications of the subject matter. For instance, information for the air accident investigation was obtained in part from discussions with experienced accident investigators as to the problems they encountered when managing an enquiry (Rolfe and Taylor, 1984, p 150).

Associated with defining the nature and scope of the problem is the identification of participant roles. Clarification of each role in a team exercise is particularly important to avoid the possibility of 'spectator roles'. Also, the roles establish the broad parameters for the interactions that occur in the exercise. Moreover, a group of four or five students should not be simply introduced to a problem; the risk is that allocating responsibilities and avoiding conflicts may become a major focus of the exercise.

Some simulations have a natural sequence of events. In the archaeological simulation, team members first sift the soil and identify the fragments they find. Then each member, in his or her role as a bone expert, lithics expert, etc., conducts the appropriate analyses and writes a section of the final report. The role of the crew chief is to provide assistance where needed and to edit and organize the final report.

In such a situation, the major task for the developer is that of constructing a rich database for study. The archaeological 'site' developed by Rice (1985), for example, is an upper palaeolithic rock shelter site that contains the debris of nine successive cultural groups and spans an extended period of time from 50 000 to 8 000 years ago.

If the participants are not to interact physically with the problem site, then the developers must determine in what ways the participants are to gain access to data. A work setting may be established for the simulation, such as a command centre, office, or laboratory. In the air accident investigation, Rolfe and Taylor (1984) established an office for the team with a secretary and telephone. The team requests data and reports from officials and others at the accident site through the secretary.

However, participants cannot be left to their own devices simply to request reports from a secretary or other individual. Instead, some sequence of events and ongoing activity must be assured in the exercise. This task may be addressed in several ways. First, the exercise may be subdivided into time periods that are logical for the problem or task. For instance, an investigation may be divided into 'days' with an informal briefing to the team's supervisor scheduled at the end of each 'day'.

Second, participants receive introductory information that serves as a stimulus for their actions. Participants in an air accident investigation receive a role card, a staff organizational chart, a description and map of the airport where the accident occurred, a brief description of the small country in which the airport is located and photographs of the accident (Rolfe and Taylor, 1984). A written transcript of a radio interview of an eyewitness to the accident and sketchy information provided by the agency director are the core information about the accident that is provided.

Third, peripheral roles that may be taken by members of the project staff are identified and they interact periodically with the participants. Roles that may be included in an accident investigation are the night watchman, the pathologist, a newspaper reporter and the airport director. Consultants may also be viable roles, depending on the particular situation.

Fourth, staff-initiated events that precipitate participant actions are identified. For instance, a telephone call to members of an air accident investigation team about the information broadcast in a radio interview of key witnesses may be included early in the enquiry.

Fifth, events that may impede or slow down the enquiry may also be included. In the air accident investigation, for instance, demands arrive for television interviews with the deputy director and other countries with an interest in the investigation request representation at the enquiry. Developers of the simulation must also prepare for the participants taking any of several possible courses of action. If an investigation seems to be taking too long, participants may receive a copy of a current news story with a headline such as 'Investigation Stalled: Public Demands Answers'.

In addition to providing events that may precipitate participant action, the simulation also includes reactions to their decisions. Several sources of reactions to participant actions may be used in open-structure simulations. They are a) results of tests conducted on data by the participants themselves; b) information obtained from consultants; c) lists of information requested by the participants (such as reports or newspaper accounts); and d) reactions of those in peripheral roles taken by project staff.

These events are then arranged into a draft timetable and incorporated with the types of data to be made available and associated reports or tests that are to be prepared. The timetable with the associated data sources and effects serves three functions. First, it acts as the framework for developing essential materials that may be requested by participants in the simulation and for reviewing the simulation events. Second, it becomes the schedule by which the project staff monitors the simulation and inserts specified events at the appropriate time. Third, it is a guide for noting when participants fail to take account of important data essential for resolution. This information as well as appropriate choices and strategies implemented by participants is the basis for the post-simulation conferences in which participants and project staff analyse the participants' cognitive strategies.

In summary, diagnostic simulations are a versatile type of interactive exercise. Although difficult to design well, they are appropriate in a variety of subject areas and provide a type of problem-solving experience not found in other exercises.

EVALUATING DIAGNOSTIC SIMULATIONS

Step 1: Determine the type and format of the simulation.
- Is the exercise a client-management or mystery resolution simulation?
- Is the simulation a closed-structure or an open-structure exercise? If closed-structure, is the exercise developed in booklet form or is it a computer-delivered simulation?

Step 2: Analyse the nature and scope of the problem.
- Is the problem non-trivial, yet not too complex for participants to interpret?
- Is the problem an important priority for the role(s) selected for the simulation?
- Has the developer provided a context that sets the stage for investigating the problem?

Closed-structure simulations

Step 3: Evaluate the opening scene.
- Does the opening scene briefly describe the situation in concrete, yet neutral terms?
- Does the opening scene describe the physical setting of the problem, the student's role and any limitation in time, facilities or assistance available to the student? Also, does it include a minimum amount of extraneous information?
- What type of media is used to present the opening scene? (Computer screen, videotape or videodisc, audiorecording or other media?) Is the format credible?

Step 4: Evaluate the general sequence of the simulation.
- Does the exercise provide for multiple branching that

incorporates data-gathering and management phases (ie, the exercise is not linear)?

- Does the participant choose which phases are to be explored at each stage of the investigation?
- Does the exercise provide for exiting the participant for a fatal error?

Step 5: Evaluate the options and responses to the options.

- Do the sets of options include a range of choices (essential, facilitative, neutral, impeding and harmful)?
- Are the options credible (ie, incorrect options are not detectable on observation)?
- Are the options designed so that later complications arise as a result of early strategies implemented by participants?
- Are the responses to the options descriptive, but not evaluative?
- Are the responses in appropriate format, language and/or style?

Open-structure simulations

Step 3: Review the background information and setting for the simulation.

- Is the background information sufficient, yet concise?
- Is the setting for the simulation removed from the site of the problem to be investigated? If so, what means of communication with the problem site and mechanisms of data collection are to be used?
- Is the setting credible, given the nature of the problem?

Step 4: Analyse the roles.

- Is each role essential to the investigation?
- Is the responsibility of each role clearly delineated?
- Does the simulation include one or more peripheral roles? If so, what is their function?

Step 5: Review the projected sequence of events.

- Is the exercise divided into specific time periods? If so, are they credible?
- What staff-initiated events are provided in the simulation? Are they credible?
- In what ways do the peripheral roles taken by staff influence the sequence of events?
- Are impeding events planned for in the exercise? Are they credible?
- Does the simulation include a logical end point?

Step 6: Analyse the data base and reactions to possible participant actions.

- What are the types of data that will be available upon participant request?
- Does the database include correct, inconsequential and inappropriate sources of information?
- What types of simulation reactions to participant actions are included (eg, test results, newspaper reactions, communications from superiors, etc)?
- Is a broad range of simulation reactions available in the event of the participants taking an unusual course of action?

REFERENCES

Bidwell, C M, Collins-Nakai, R L, Taylor, M B and Jensen, W A (1985) 'Multidisciplinary team production of computer-based simulations to teach pediatrics', *Journal of Medical Education*, **60**, 397–403.

de Mesquita, P (1987) 'The information processing and diagnostic decision making of school psychologists while solving a computer-simulated diagnostic referral problem', paper presented at National Association of School Psychologists meeting, New Orleans, March.

Gallini, J and Gredler, M (1989) *Designing Computer-based Instruction: Applications in BASIC and Logo*, Glenview, IL: Scott, Foresman.

Jones, G L and Keith, K D (1983) 'Computer clinical simulations in the health sciences', *Journal of Computer-based Instruction*, **9**, 3, 108–14.

McGuire, C, Solomon, L M and Bashook, P G (1975) *Construction and Use of Written Simulations*, Houston, TX: The Psychological Corporation.

McKelvie, J (1978) 'Simulations in police training', *Sagset*, **8**, 1, 15–19.

Miller, E J (1990) 'In videodisc veritas: Interactive video at Harvard Law School', *T. H. E. Journal*, March, 78–80.

Pickell, G C, Medal, D, Mann, W S and Staebler, R J (1986) 'Computerizing clinical patient problems: An evolving tool for medical education', *Medical Education*, **20**, 201–3.

Rice, P C (1985) 'Using a simulated site to teach data analysis in archeology', *Anthropology and Education Quarterly*, **16**, 4, 301–5.

Rolfe, J and Taylor, F (1984) 'IN THE HOT SEAT: An accident investigation management simulation', in Jaques, D and Tipper, E (eds) *Learning for the Future with Games and Simulations*, 149–64, Loughborough: SAGSET/ Loughborough University of Technology.

Willems, J (1981) 'Problem-based (group) teaching: A cognitive science approach to using available knowledge', *Instructional Science*, **10**, 5–21.

Wynn, R (1964) 'Simulations: Terrible reality in the preparation of school administrators', *Phi Delta Kappan*, **46**, 170–73.

6 Crisis-management simulations

In the decade that followed World War II, the uncertainties of the cold war and 'the bomb' gave birth to a new kind of interactive exercise. Referred to first as 'crisis games' and then as 'political–military exercises', they presented the participants with an international crisis in the form of a scenario. The participants, representing officials of different countries, attempted to resolve the situation with minimal negative side-effects and consequences within the constraints established by the rules. In these exercises, resolution of the problem required negotiation and compromise – key elements in the development of foreign policy.

These exercises indicated the *potential* of simulations in which participants could experience the rapid unfolding of events and the pressures for quick decision-making that a crisis precipitates. However, decision-making in the exercises proceeded slowly. The analysis of policy rather than the experience of developing rapid responses to an impending threat was the focus. Thus, the development of crisis-management simulations remains, for the most part, an unexplored topic.

OVERVIEW

The crisis-management simulation is an exercise in which teams of individuals allocate resources in an effort to avert or minimize an impending threat or danger to a business, social service, industry, or a social, economic or political system. Issues germane to the design of crisis-management simulations are the characteristics of the original 'crisis games', the nature of crisis situations and the essential characteristics of crisis-management simulations.

Early developments

The first 'crisis game' (so-called by early developers) was designed by Herbert Goldhammer, a social scientist at Rand Corporation. Known as 'The cold war game', the exercise addressed international crises in the context of the threat of overt hostilities between the USA and the USSR.

'The cold war game' was soon followed by a series of exercises developed at MIT by Lincoln Bloomfield. Referred to as 'Polex' – for political exercises – each involved a local or regional event that represented a possible threat to the status quo in international relations. The first exercise involved a Polish nationalist uprising similar to the 1956 Hungarian revolt and one in 1960 examined the collapse of the Shah of Iran (Allen, 1987). Also included in the series were the emergence of a pro-Castro government in Venezuela, insurgency in India, internal strife in Angola and Chinese penetration into Burma (Allen, 1987, p 152).

From two to five teams typically participated in these exercises, including a US and Soviet team. One team represented 'Nature' which was renamed 'Control' in the 'Polex' exercises. The Control group had several functions (Bloomfield and Whaley, 1965, p 858). First, they introduced unexpected events that occur in the real world, but are not controlled by particular countries. Included are the death of world figures, famines and so on.

Second, they served as umpires, ruling on the plausibility of moves, thus requiring teams to live within the implications of their selected strategies. Third, since only a small portion of the political world could be represented by the teams, Control provided necessary inputs on behalf of other nations or international organizations whose actions may be relevant to the crisis or to which the teams are sending messages. Fourth, Control was permitted to leak accurate or distorted versions of classified information to the media (Allen, 1987).

Each team was assigned to a separate room and provided with a secretary–typist. The exercise was initiated with a 'Scenario-Problem' that specified prior history, capabilities and military dispositions. The document concluded with the unfolding crisis situation up to the beginning of the exercise (Bloomfield and Whaley, 1965, p 860). The exercise then proceeded through a series of discontinuous move periods that ranged from three to six (the number determined by Control in light of emerging events). During the exercise, Control also determined the relationship between real time and simulated time, with simulated time ranging from 8 to 195 days. Intensity of the crisis, the complexity of negotiations in formulating responses to the crisis, and the speed with which escalation may have developed, influenced the time span set by Control.

Each move period began with inputs from Control, followed by one and a half to three hours in which each team defined and redefined its basic strategies, assessed the motives underlying the moves of other teams, tried to predict future events and then determined their moves. Then one team member typically briefed Control (separately from other briefings) so that Control could commence work without waiting for detailed documents. The exception was 'hot-line' messages which were delivered immediately (Bloomfield and Whaley, 1965, p 860).

Actions taken by the teams were thus highly stylized. Interactions among the teams were in writing and were submitted first to Control who reviewed them for plausibility and then passed them on to the appropriate 'country'.

Although these early exercises were referred to as crisis games, their main goal was policy analysis. That is, in most cases, the initial crisis merely served as a catalyst for the development of policy. Goldhammer and Speier (1959) viewed the purpose of these exercises as intellectual collaboration. The most valuable feature, in their view, was the verbal or written discussion of political problems that developed during the exercise. Goldhammer also suggested that recesses should sometimes be called when ideas reached a particularly interesting point in order to give the teams time to discuss and think about the developments.

Recently, some policy analysis exercises have been developed and implemented through computer networking. Participants in various countries receive messages from Control and send messages in return by electronic mail (see Neal *et al.*, 1987). The conferencing capabilities of the system make it possible to bring sets of teams together in real-time interactions. Because the participants are drawn from around the world, the issues and complexities that arise reflect the characteristics of current international political realities.

Like the early foreign policy exercises, one purpose of the computer networking exercises is that of policy analysis. Another major interest is that of underlying questions of international relations theory (Neal *et al.*, p 18). Therefore, these exercises do not purport to represent crisis exercises in terms of participants experiencing the threat, tension and escalating time pressures associated with a crisis.

The nature of crisis situations

Designing or evaluating a crisis simulation depends in part on an understanding of the differences between a crisis and other problems or tasks. Some analysts define the term 'crisis', which comes from the Greek *krinein* (to separate), as the critical turning or branching point in some human activity (Hermann, 1969). This usage is common in the medical field, in which references are made to the crisis point in a patient's battle against a life-threatening or debilitating disease.

The difficulty in relying on the concept of a turning point as a definition is that often the critical moment cannot be determined until after the crisis has been averted or terminated. In the 1962 Cuban missile crisis, for example, the US government discovered that the Soviet Union was building missile bases on Cuba, which is 90 miles from the US mainland. The critical moment was the US establishment of a blockade on Cuba which prevented Soviet ships from delivering their cargoes to the island. Following that turning point, bargaining took place which resulted in several agreements. Moreover, after the blockade, the perceptions of each adversary of the other became less charged with negative affect (Hermann, 1969). However, until the situation came to an end, the particular turning point or decisive moment could not be identified.

Similarly, in the 1991 failed coup by Soviet communist conservatives, the critical moment occurred when KGB troops did not follow orders to fire on Russian citizens defending the Parliament building in Moscow and the Russian president. However, this critical 'turning point' was identified only in post-coup analyses of the events.

Another approach to defining a crisis is to determine the essential characteristics of a crisis situation. Analyses of various foreign policy situations indicate that certain traits or characteristics are common to situations identified as crises. Included are the need for action decisions, a sense of threat perceived by the decision-makers, an increase in uncertainties, urgency and time pressures and a sense that the outcome will shape the future (Wiener and Kahn, 1962, p 11). In other words, decision-makers perceive an impending danger accompanied by a sense of limited time to 'stop the runaway train'. These traits, however, describe the reactions of decision-makers to the situation; they do not describe the nature of the crisis itself.

Three traits imbedded in the situation denote a crisis. Specifically, a crisis a) threatens the high-priority goals of a decision-making unit; b) restricts the time available for reaction before the situation is transformed; and c) surprises the members of the decision-making unit when it takes place (Hermann, 1969, p 29).

The third characteristic, surprise, does not refer to the lack of routinized procedures for addressing the situation. It merely refers to the lack of awareness by decision-makers that the situation was about to occur. For example, nuclear power stations maintain exact replicas of their control rooms for use in training. Workers placed in the replicated control room may be faced with any combination of a variety of warning signals and readings (programmed into the computer that is directing the exercise). The readings indicate a threatening situation in which limited decision time is available for correction. Although routinized procedures exist for addressing such emergencies, the situation evokes surprise because the workers are unable to predict the particular emergency in advance.

These characteristics of a crisis situation rule out extended strategy planning as a means of resolving the situation. Instead, decision-makers must accurately assess the situation as quickly as possible while they are also considering ways to apply available resources. The third step, the allocation of resources, is also accompanied by periodic re-assessment to determine whether changes in response are needed.

Types of crisis situations

The various ways in which the basic steps of crisis-management are executed depend in part on the scope and nature of the particular crisis.

First, the crisis may be local, regional, national or international For example, natural disasters, such as floods or tornadoes, may be local or regional in scope, Epidemics, such as cholera, may range from local to international. The implication for designing crisis-management simulations is that the broader the scope of the problem, the greater the number of variables that will influence the situation in unpredictable ways.

The nature of the crisis, in terms of implications for design, may be determined by classifying crisis situations by the characteristics of threat, decision time before the situation changes and surprise. Each of these characteristics may be viewed as a continuum in which a crisis situation may be located. That is, situations may vary from low to high threat, low to high degree of surprise and brief to extended time for decision-makers to avert or alleviate the crisis.

For example, the AIDS epidemic, an ongoing crisis, is viewed by medical researchers as a high threat to the goals and well-being of society. This crisis was also predictable (low surprise) when the nature and virulence of the disease were first discovered.

However, the AIDS epidemic is not viewed as a high-threat crisis by all groups in society. The funds and resources allocated to education and other efforts to stop its spread indicate that, compared to other problems, AIDS is perceived by governments as a moderate threat to society as a whole. The implication of these different perceptions for the design of crisis-management simulations is that decision-making roles must be selected carefully. That is, the crisis presented in the exercise cannot be perceived by the decision-makers in the simulation as a low-threat situation.

In addition to the three basic dimensions, crisis situations are also characterized by incomplete and/or distorted information. Managing natural disasters such as floods or earthquakes, for instance, is accompanied by confused information from several sources. In other crisis situations, essential information may be lacking. For instance, a hospital autopsy report may suggest (without proof) that tainted antibiotics are a likely cause of the complications in two deaths.

Characteristics of crisis-management simulations

Like the diagnostic simulation, crisis-management simulations also have an opening scene, participant requests for information, actions taken by participants and reactions to participant decisions. However, there are several differences between the two types. First, the situation presented in the brief scenario in the crisis-management simulation is perceived as a threat by the participants. For example, in a natural disaster, citizens' lives are disrupted and the normal life of the community becomes dysfunctional. Community leaders are threatened if some tranquility and degree of normality is not quickly restored.

Similarly, a computer malfunction in a stockbroker's office threatens loss of clients for the company if not detected and corrected quickly.

A second difference is that the time available for data-gathering and applying solutions is severely limited in the crisis-management simulation. Without an adequate response by the decision-makers, the crisis will become more acute and/or extensive. A resolution may be needed in minutes, as in a nuclear power reactor, or it may span a few weeks (in simulated time) if the situation is one in which the consequences of some participant decisions are not immediately known. In a natural disaster that produces disease and death, for example, these consequences will continue beyond a few days.

Third, to be effective, a crisis-management simulation should produce the same reactions and feelings in the participants as the experience of handling a crisis in their everyday lives. Included are tension, uncertainty, time pressures and a sense of inadequate information and frustration. Therefore, the crisis selected for the simulation should not be one perceived to be a low-threat, low-surprise event that may be resolved over a period of time.

Crisis-management simulations are typically open-structure exercises in which a team addresses an impending emergency. An example is the simulation *Atlantis* (Ritchie, 1985) which addresses the complexities in managing relief operations after a natural or industrial disaster.

Examples of closed-structure simulations are the control room crises used in nuclear power stations (described on p. 79). The computer program initiates any of several emergencies by changing the readings on key indicators. The program also responds to worker actions by further changes in the settings. These simulations are used both for training and assessment.

Crisis-management simulations in which the participants interact exclusively with a computer are not recommended. The problem is, of course, maintaining reality of function for the participants. Computers are not the root cause of crisis situations (unless, of course, they crash). Thus, the possible disadvantages of a computer-delivered exercise for crisis-management simulations are a) the lack of interaction among decision-makers; b) the false sense that time is not a variable; and c) the possibility that the exercise will be perceived as a game.

Crisis-management simulations may be used in a variety of settings. However, an important role for these exercises is yet to be fully realized: that of providing opportunities for students in a variety of subject areas to experience the complexity, tension, uneasiness and the sense of inadequate information that accompanies resolving a crisis in any setting.

In other words, real-world problems do not present themselves in textbook form. Instead, they often disrupt an important process or activity and information about the probable circumstances may be sketchy. For example, an important skill in computer programming is to be able to 'debug' programs. Creating a situation in which a small stockbroking company is about to lose clients through the malfunctioning of its computer system establishes a non-textbook crisis for programmers and accountants to resolve.

MAJOR DESIGN ISSUES

Several issues are important in the design of crisis-management simulations. Included are the differences between social situations and crisis-management, the design of simulation components and the interaction of those components to produce tension and a sense of threat in the participants.

Social situations and crisis management

When considering a social or political framework as the setting for a simulation, the designer should be clear about the purpose. That is, is the emphasis in the exercise resource allocation to avert a crisis or the insights to be gained by participants through negotiation and interaction with other participants representing states, provinces, or countries as they attempt to achieve their goals? If the answer is the second option, then the exercise is intended to be a social-system simulation, not a crisis-management simulation.

This decision is critical, because the designation of roles, the interactions of the participants and other factors are executed in different ways for the two types. If the decision as to type cannot be clearly made, the result can be an exercise that is not successful in meeting the goals of either type.

Consider the situation in which the selected crisis situation is a computer malfunction in a stockbroker's office. The malfunction jeopardizes sales and trading opportunities and threatens the loss of clients through the company's inability to provide accurate information and to respond to client requests. The exercise may be developed as a crisis-management simulation, for example, if the purpose is to restore customer confidence quickly. Available resources include print-outs of the previous week's transactions for each sales person and a listing of the computer commands in the programs that encode, transform, store and retrieve the data entered by the employees. In addition, the decision-makers selected to address the problem are accountants, sales representatives and computer programmers.

In contrast, the simulation becomes a different type of exercise if the basic elements are changed. For example, the goal may be altered to that of identifying a culprit responsible for the malfunction. The president of the company, the head of the accounting department and the sales manager may be added to the group of participants. Added to the available resources are the employee time records for the previous week. These key changes alter the exercise into one that is highly charged with the potential for conflict among the participants. It is no longer the allocation of intellectual and/or material resources to resolve a crisis for the company.

Another example of an exercise that failed to produce the intended effects is described by Cohen (1962). Ninety students, drawn from two undergraduate classes in political science at the University of Wisconsin participated in the exercise. The students represented 5 to 6 officials of 8 countries and 45 US officials (all major foreign policy-making offices, an 11-person Congress and a 9-person CIA).

The 'crisis' in the foreign policy exercise was that Iraq was attempting to force Syria out of the United Arab Republic. However, the students summarily dispensed with the conflict in order to be free to follow their own designs. In other words, the 'simulation' became a role-playing free-wheeling exercise. Some players, for example, complained about the time required to read the world newspaper, which contained important information about new events impinging on countries in the simulation. Instead, they could scarcely wait to 'get back in the ring' of negotiations (Cohen, 1962).

Several factors contributed to the implementation problems of the exercise. First, the exercise followed the format of the early foreign policy exercises – long planning periods followed by a single move by each team. The college students, unlike state department officials, had little incentive to explore the finer points of foreign policy development within this structure.

Second, the so-called crisis situation was not a threat to the major decision-makers. Negative effects to the USA were not perceived as escalating from the situation. Third, part of the implementation difficulties were also attributable to the lack of contingencies in the exercise for different participant behaviours. That is, failure to attend to an important action by another country should have resulted in at least minor negative consequences.

Establishing the crisis climate

An effective crisis-management simulation is achieved through careful attention to several factors that contribute to a climate of crisis. In addition to selecting a bona fide crisis situation, other factors are the decision-making roles and simulation events that contribute to an increasing sense of urgency for the participants.

The selected crisis

The 'ideal' combination of characteristics to establish tension and uncertainty initially is a high-threat, high-surprise situation that must be resolved fairly quickly to avert disaster. For example, a train loaded with toxic chemicals reports that the brake system has failed and it is headed for a large city in a valley at the foot of a mountain. The decision-making roles selected for the exercise are those of members of a disaster management team.

The scope of the crisis is also important in the design of a credible exercise. Crises limited to a particular locale, such as a business, a school or a hospital are accompanied by a restricted set of potential roles likely to be involved in resolving the situation. As the scope of the crisis expands, ie, community, region or nation, the developer is faced with the problem of an increasing number of decision-makers that may interact with the situation and an expanded set of variables that may influence the situation in unpredictable ways.

One solution is to propose a crisis with a potentially broad impact that is known only to a few decision-makers. For example, a hospital administrator and the department heads have been informed that two patient deaths may be the result of complications induced by tainted antibiotics. In the simulation, the reactions of members of the board of trustees and others who learn of the crisis may be handled in the form of messages to the hospital staff.

The decision-makers
Roles should be established for participants in which they *directly* experience the effects of an unresolved crisis. In other words, selecting roles with power and prestige is not sufficient to ensure that participants will experience reality of function. Therefore, the decision-makers should be those individuals that clearly have a vested interest in the outcome. 'The situation threatens *their* goals, it surprises *them*, and it is *they* who are faced with a short decision time' (Hermann, 1969, p 34).

An example is a scenario in which a country is facing a trade embargo from an industrial competitor in the world market. The crisis threatens jobs in shipping and industry as well as the loss of the next election by the party in power. In such a situation, the minister of trade, the prime minister (accused by the opposition party as the cause of the problem) and their advisors are likely to become involved in deploying resources to resolve the crisis.

Events in the simulation
Like the team diagnostic simulation, the crisis-management simulation is an open-structure exercise. Therefore, some organization and sequence should be imposed on the simulation by the designers.

The early foreign-policy exercises made use of a control team that reviewed actions to keep the teams on course and which also masterminded other events to take place in the simulation. The use of an omnipresent control team, however, is not recommended because it detracts from reality of function for the simulation participants.

Instead, the elements described in Chapter 5 for diagnostic simulations may be used to provide periodic input in crisis-management exercises. They include one or two peripheral roles taken by members of project staff, messages from others, staff-initiated events and subdividing the time period into 'days' or 'hours'. However, other elements are also necessary to produce the 'run-away train' effect essential to a crisis-management simulation.

The management of time is particularly important to enhance the sense of threat. The developers of *Atlantis*, a disaster-management simulation, divided the time into three phases (Ritchie, 1985, p 36). Phase 1 is the period immediately after the disaster. Participants are gathering and organizing information about the event and establishing the availability and location of resources required to meet the crisis. Phase 1 runs in real time because participants are receiving more information than they can handle.

In phase 2, distinct time periods are used to represent 24 hours of real time. Also, as phase 2 progresses, these time periods become shorter (Ritchie, 1985). One purpose is for participants to experience the consequences of any errors in preventive action in the early 'days' of the exercise. That is, injured and ill individuals who did not receive treatment in the early days begin to die. Phase 3 introduces logistical problems and the integration of foreign relief contributions with national resources (Ritchie, 1985).

Another important factor is incomplete or distorted information. Depending on the nature of the crisis, broken communication lines that result in incomplete data may be appropriate, or two 'teams' responsible for assessing the situation may be submitting conflicting reports to the participants in the simulation. Meanwhile, participants are receiving urgent messages from officials and others to resolve the situation quickly.

A third factor is that some influences in a crisis operate in concert while others are in conflict (Ritchie, 1985, p 95). In the crisis involving tainted antibiotics, for example, the urgent need for information on antibiotic supplies on the different floors and in the pharmacy conflicts with the need for preventing panic.

Providing a complex problem with decreasing time to solve it is not sufficient to label an interactive exercise as a crisis-management simulation. An example is *The Crisis Game* (Friman, 1991). In the middle of a class lecture or discussion, the instructor announces the occurrence of a 'crisis'. Students are divided into groups of 5–10 and given information packets. They are instructed to develop a policy recommendation within a specified time frame, typically 20–30 minutes. Then the instructor, over the next several minutes, interrupts the group at different intervals from 1 to 5 minutes with new information. The information either affects the stated crisis or is irrelevant. Then when 5–10 minutes remain of the original time frame, the instructor announces that an emergency press conference is scheduled in 5 minutes and recommendations must be completed at that time. The instructor announces the remaining time at 30-second intervals. At the conclusion of the exercise, each group chooses a spokesperson to present and defend the group's policies before the class.

This exercise is useful in undergraduate international relations classes for illustrating some of the aspects of decision-making in foreign policy. (*The Crisis Game* is discussed further in Chapter 8.) The participants are faced with time pressures and inadequate information as they develop their recommendations. However, the participants are not managing a crisis. They are simply developing recommendations for government policy. In a crisis-management simulation, participants experience the consequences of their decisions as they attempt to manage a situation that borders on being out of control.

Moreover, reality of function in a crisis-management simulation also depends on the sense of threat experienced by the decision-makers which includes more than increasing time pressure. Finally, events in *The Crisis Game* that precipitate the sense of time pressure are all clearly arbitrary and each is announced by the instructor. In a crisis-management simulation, events evolve from the nature of the crisis itself and the decisions made by participants.

Crisis-management simulations are not easy to design. Developing events that create the appropriate climate requires attention to several factors, all of which interact to produce the desired effect.

EVALUATING CRISIS-MANAGEMENT SIMULATIONS

Step 1: Analyse the crisis situation.
- Do the background information and opening scene convey a sense of extreme urgency?
- Does the crisis specifically threaten the decision-makers in the simulation?
- What is the scope of the crisis?

Step 2: Review the decision-making roles.
- Are the decision-makers empowered to resolve the crisis?
- Is a role assigned to each participant that is not a spectator role?
- Is the crisis a high-threat situation for the decision-makers?

Step 3: Evaluate the dynamics of the exercise.
- Do the participants experience the effects of their decisions?
- Do events evolve from the nature of the crisis rather than arbitrary decisions by the director?
- Do the participants experience increased time pressure?
- Is incomplete or distorted information a factor in the exercise?

- Do events (such as those provided by peripheral roles) accelerate as the exercise progresses?

REFERENCES

Allen, T B (1987) *War Games*, New York: McGraw-Hill.

Bloomfield, L P and Whaley, B (1965) 'The political–military exercise: A progress report', *Orbis*, **8**, 4, 854–70.

Brewer, G D and Shubik, M (1968) *The War Game*, Cambridge, Mass: Harvard University Press.

Cohen, B C (1962) 'Political gaming in the classroom', *The Journal of Politics*, **24**, 367–81.

Friman, H R (1991) 'The Crisis Game', *Simulation and Gaming*, **22**, 1, 382–8.

Goldhammer, H and Speier, H (1959) 'Some observations on political gaming', *World Politics*, **12**, 1, 71–83.

Hermann, C F (1969) *Crises in Foreign Policy: A Simulation Analysis*, Indianapolis, Ind.: Bobbs–Merrill.

Neal, R C, Crookall, D, Wilkenfeld, J and Schapira, L (1987) 'Network gaming; A vehicle for intercultural communication', in Crookall, D, Greenblat, C S, Coote, A, Klabbers, J and Watson, D (eds) *Simulation-Gaming in the late 1980s*, 5–21, Oxford: Pergamon.

Ritchie, G (1985) 'Atlantis: The basis for management simulation development', *Simulation/Games for Learning*, **15**, 1, 28–43.

Wiener, A J and Kahn, H (1962) *Crisis and Arms Control*, New York: Hudson Institute.

Wolfenstein, E V (1967) 'Some psychological aspects of crisis leaders', in L J Edinger (ed) *Political Leadership in Industrialized Societies*, New York: Wiley.

Young, O R (1967) *The Intermediaries: Third Parties in International Crises*, Princeton NJ: Princeton University Press.

7 Data-management simulations

Data management is a fact of life in complex societies. Individuals plan personal budgets, balance their cheque-books, and interpret stock market reports in planning and evaluating their investments. Similarly, businesses, institutions and agencies evaluate and monitor various types of data in their efforts to achieve particular goals.

Data-management simulations incorporate problems in which the participant manipulates variables that can be quantified. Assuming a role on a financial management team or that of an historical figure, for example, the participant attempts to improve the status of an organization, institution, country or individual by managing financial or economic variables.

OVERVIEW

Data-management simulations, like diagnostic simulations, have been developed in two formats. They may be either closed-structure simulations for individual roles or open-structure simulations for team decision-making.

Early developments

The antecedents of the team simulation in business is the war game. Developed in the 1600s, war games became exercises for planning strategy in the mid-1800s. From that time on, they have been a major component in military training and planning for all the major western powers.

The development of military simulations that addressed important management decisions and the advent of high-speed computers led to the development of management training exercises in business. An example developed in the early 1950s is the simulation *Monopologs*. Participants functioned as inventory managers in a simplified version of the Air Force supply system (Faria, 1987).

The first management training exercise was developed by the American Management Association in 1956 and was known as the *Top Management Decision Simulation*. It became the prototype for the large number of interactive business exercises in current use. Company decisions for each team were fed into an IBM 650 computer. The computer calculated the effects of each group's decisions according to predetermined mathematical models and the results, including balance sheets, were given to each team. Each group reviewed its decisions, attempted to guess the opponent's strategies and made new decisions for the next business quarter. The exercise continued in this way for several business quarters, each of which required approximately an hour (Tansey and Unwin, 1969, p 4). Characteristics of this prototype, however, have led to implementation problems in current exercises referred to as business games. These problems are discussed in the section 'open-structure simulations'.

An early example of the historically-based individual exercise was developed in the early 1960s by two employees of IBM (Carlson, 1969). Known as *The Sumerian Game*, the computer-delivered simulation is an example of the closed-structure format. The exercise was designed to teach 11-year-olds some economic principles of a neolithic revolution in Mesopotamia in 3500 BC. A programmed tape and slide presentation introduced the student, who assumed the role of Luduga I, priest–ruler of Lagash, to the situation.

The student then made decisions about the amount of grain to plant for the year, the amount to be saved and the amount to be given to the people for food. Twice yearly the Royal Steward, Uraba (the computer), reported the economic condition of the kingdom (Wing, 1968).

As the exercise continued, the student was faced with a variety of problems. For example, grain can only be stored for short periods before rotting and destruction by rodents occurs. Other problems included expanding population, irrigation and foreign trade. In addition, the exercise randomly introduced disasters such as floods, granary fires and so on, to which the student was required to respond. The computer then reacted by recording changes in economic development consistent with the student's decisions (Carlson, 1969).

The exercise also became more difficult as it progressed. In the first phase, the student attempted to solve the problems of an agricultural economy. However, in the second phase, the goal was to apply surplus grain to the development of crafts. In other words, the city–state must first survive some early crises and then begin to build a small grain surplus as well as to increase the population and maintain a high rate of technological innovation (Carlson, 1969).

The exercise made use of three IBM 1050 terminals. Two terminals were equipped with modified carousel projectors and the third with an experimental random-access filmstrip projector. Approximately 75 pictures were projected at appropriate times during each exercise. Of interest is that this use of technology was an effort to achieve what is now accomplished by random access CD-ROM technology.

Major characteristics

Three major features characterize data-management simulations. First, as already mentioned, the focus is on the interrelationships and trade-offs among measurable variables. In *Interbank*, an exercise in bank management, participants explore the interrelationships among profitability, liquidity and solvency and between profits and volume of business (Galitz, 1983).

The second characteristic is that the task for participants is to allocate available resources in order to achieve a particular economic goal. In *The Sumerian Game*, for instance, the priest–king made decisions about the disposition of each year's crop of grain. The long-range goal was both to provide for the people and to improve the trading status of Mesopotamia. One limitation of that exercise, however, is that the participant only manipulated one variable – the annual harvest. Thus, the exercise risked becoming tedious for the participant.

In data-management simulations, changes made in one variable influence the status of one or more other variables. Therefore, the third characteristic is that data-management simulations are based on mathematical models. The particular model specifies the increase or decrease in particular variables as other variables are altered.

In single-participant simulations, the student takes the role of an individual in a particular historical period or a particular context. In that role, the participant makes decisions over a period of time with the goal of improving the status of the individual or the country, institution or system for which that individual is responsible. Team-based simulations, in contrast, are open-structure exercises that involve the management of a company, bank or other institution or organization through several business cycles.

Data-management simulations are similar to both diagnostic and crisis-management simulations in two characteristics. First, the exercise should provide for flexibility of decision-making. In *Interbank*, for example, team decisions are made in five general categories: lending, deposits, investments, corporate operations and general. Examples of some of the decisions in these areas are spreading retail lending across several sectors or specializing in a few; securing maximum return from investments or managing investments to provide sufficient liquidity (a passive strategy); expanding or reducing branch networks; and determining the ultimate size of the bank (Galitz, 1983).

Second, the process should be controllable by the participants (Galitz, 1983). As indicated in Chapter 4, the exercise should not be dominated by random events. In several exercises developed for elementary and secondary school classrooms, however, random events control the outcomes. An example is the computer exercise *Oregon Trail*, in which participants are supposedly travelling West by wagon train. However, the outcome is completely controlled by chance mishaps. Participants are continually confronted by a variety of disasters that are translated by the computer model into the depletion of ammunition, food and miscellaneous supplies. The dominance of these events led one student to remark, 'You can't ever win; you always seem to lose' (Fisher, 1982).

MAJOR DESIGN ISSUES

Two key issues in the design of data-management simulations are a) the specification of the mathematical model, and b) the identification of the major decisions to be made by the participants.

Specification of the mathematical model

Identification of the major constructs to be included in the simulation and the empirical relationships among them is the foundation of the simulation. To the extent that the model is not well specified, the resulting exercise will be at best superficial and uninformative for the participants.

Microcomputer spreadsheet programs, such as Lotus1-2-3, are well suited to developing the mathematical model for an exercise that will adjust parameter values as student inputs are made. The task for the designer is to specify the set of equations that reflect the relationships among the variables. In one prototype economic model for a country, for example, 12 equations describe domestic demand, the economy's supply potential and the international component (imports and exports). In the international component, balance of payments (BP) = Xbar*P-IM*Pfbar*Ebar where Xbar = exports, P = price level, IM = imports, Pfbar = world prices and Ebar = exchange rate. Equations are also included for imports (IM) and price level (P) (Adams and Geczy, 1991).

One potential danger in designing data-management simulations is that of quantifying the unquantifiable. Many problems encountered in the classical sciences, engineering and accounting are rigorously quantifiable, and mathematical formulas can provide clear-cut representations of such problems (Ginter and Rucks, 1983, p 18). However, the danger in other fields is that 'a squishy problem may be given a mathematical form that appears to be an unambiguous representation of a real world problem; but this appearance is often superficial and may evaporate rapidly when probed' (ibid).

An example is the computer exercise *The Would-Be Gentleman*, discussed in Chapter 3. In that exercise, the player takes the role of the eldest son and makes investment decisions and decisions about marriage, making a will and finding a protector. Two characteristics of the exercise place it in the game category. One is the objective, which is to earn the highest score. The other is the quantification of social status with the goal of achieving the highest possible score. Financial decisions in the France of Louis XIV were closely related to social standing. However, the relationship was not formula-based.

The mathematical model that is the foundation for the simulation should also be logical and credible to the participants. Therefore, the behaviour of the process must make sense to them, that is, the relationships specified among the variables should be consistent and, in the long run, predictable (given no major catastrophe). For example, in the exercise *Oregon Trail*, a broken leg is translated by the mathematical model into $20 subtracted from the student's resources in 'miscellaneous supplies'. No empirical relationship, however, exists between the occurrence of a broken leg and an expenditure of $20.

If the mathematical relationships specified in the model are not predictable in the long run, then participants cannot be successful. Such a situation violates the basic purpose of tactical-decision simulations which is to apply an area of expertise in data interpretation and management.

Development of the decision model

In diagnostic and crisis-management simulations, participants are able to follow any of several lines of enquiry and strategies to resolve the presented problem. The basic context of these simulations, in which participants are expected to discover the nature and/or extent of a particular problem, lends itself to providing flexibility in decision-making for the participants.

Data-management simulations, however, present two problems for the designer in establishing the decision-making situations for participants. One is that of providing a comprehensive array of variables for participants to address. This problem is related to the specification of variables and their relationships. If the model specifies only a few relationships involving two or three variables, then participants are functioning in a restricted setting.

Furthermore, one purpose of tactical-decision simulations is to permit students to apply strategies in organizing, interpreting and manipulating data. A restricted set of decisions does not provide these opportunities. The exercise *Lemonade Stand*, for example, allows students only three decisions which are made repeatedly. They are a) the number of glasses of lemonade they wish to sell; b) the price per glass; and c) the amount to be spent on advertising. (Other problems with this exercise are discussed later in this chapter.)

In contrast, the simulation, *Interbank*, as indicated earlier, includes decisions made in five broad categories. Furthermore, the decisions within the categories are fairly involved, eg, to spread retail lending across several sectors or to specialize in a few areas. In order to address the array of decisions, each 'company', prior to the first period of operation, draws up a corporate plan that states their goals and outlines a set of strategies to accomplish the goals.

Evaluating student performance

Like diagnostic and crisis-management simulations, data-management simulations should evaluate the strategies implemented by participants for strengths and weaknesses. However, the simulations developed for use in business establish competitive situations among hypothetical companies or financial institutions. Winners and losers in the exercise are determined according to performance on one outcome – the profitability of the company or institution that the participants are managing. Profit is interpreted as actual profit, return on equity, return on investment, stock price, inventory turnover or even market share (Teach, 1990, p 12).

Several problems may be identified with the use of profit as the criterion for evaluation. First, since most management exercises are conducted for 8 to 16 cycles of decision-making, participants implement strategies to enhance short-term profits at the expense of long-term profitability. Thus, the exercise, by determining large portions of a student's grade on short-term profits, sends the message that management has a very short horizon (Teach, 1990, p 15).

Second, the practice of identifying winners and losers on the basis of profits has generated a variety of behaviours that are counterproductive to learning (often stated as the goal of the exercises). Among them are desperations plays, such as charging an astronomical price for a product in the hopes of selling a few, and end-of-activity plays, such as eliminating all R & D or ordering no raw materials (Teach, 1990, p 16). In addition, some participants become excessively competitive throughout the exercise and 'treat the game as a game only, a challenge, an opportunity to show their prowess by beating other teams' (Lundy, 1985, p 30). Golden and Smith (1991) describe such teams as 'dogfighters' because their behaviour 'resembles the classic World War II aviation dogfight' (p 85). However, companies such as IBM and Coca Cola are not evaluated in the real world in terms of which company outperforms the other.

Another problem associated with the competitive exercises is that some teams tend to not participate in the activity. Lundy (1985) refers to such teams as RHINO (Really Here In Name Only). They are the 15–20 per cent 'who "opt out" either physically or mentally' (p 31). Golden and Smith (1991) describe some teams as having an interest in the exercise, but lacking in the energy to pursue the winner's circle (p 84). These teams attend only to the pro forma aspects of the exercise, such as the deadlines for submitting reports. Also, some teams report that in the last few quarters they could not improve their company's performance; thus, they just went through the motions (Lundy, 1985, p

29). Furthermore, the designation of winners and losers is counterproductive to producing the review of one's strategies that is essential to learning. Lundy (1985) notes that not only are the losers disappointed, but the winners tend to not question their own decisions or the inadvertent 'help' they received from other teams.

Some simulations incorporate mechanisms to discourage unreasonable or extreme efforts to boost profits or to derail another company. The *Interbank* exercise, for example, counters the tendency for teams to make extreme decisions in efforts to corner the market in two ways. First, a number of background teams are included that are managed by the computer (Galitz, 1983). Also, the background teams are programmed to manage their financial institutions in a mildly aggressive manner. Their presence dilutes the impact of extreme decisions that may be taken by one or more of the active teams (Galitz, 1983, p 374). Second, the mathematical model includes a competitiveness factor (CF) that is used to modify the impact of a particular decision on the bank's position.

Although the effects of extreme decisions may be mitigated by various measures, the basic problem is that of devising an exercise that identifies teams as winners or losers. The purpose of tactical-decision simulations, however, is for individuals to apply their cognitive strategies to various types of data interpretation and management problems. Therefore, evaluating student performance should involve the strategies used by participants and not the outcomes. Teach (1991, p 20) suggests evaluating participants' working papers. In other words, a team that is able to forecast accurately direct manufacturing costs, inventory levels, market shares and so on is likely to be a well-managed firm. Also, the use of such measures does not require equal assets or marketability of products.

Learning from a simulation experience and competing with others to be a winner are contradictory goals. Therefore, establishing bona fide criteria for evaluating participant strategies also requires changing the basic paradigm of the simulation from that of designating winners and losers. Suggestions for restructuring are discussed in the following section.

TYPES OF DATA-MANAGEMENT SIMULATIONS

Data-management simulations may be constructed as pre-packaged exercises for a single participant (closed-structure format) or as team exercises (open-structure format). However, at present, many of the exercises are flawed in one or more ways.

Closed-structure simulations

Theoretically, closed-structure simulations can be designed for classroom use. At present, however, computer-delivered exercises developed for the elementary and secondary school classroom have yet to achieve the potential offered by this type of simulation.

One exercise that approximates some of the decision-making in a simulation is *The Irish Immigrant Experience*. A student takes the name of an Irish immigrant from the listings of two ships that arrived in Boston in 1840. The individual then makes decisions about jobs, housing and other budget matters. Family finances are controllable by the participants within the cost parameters operating in Boston in 1840. For example, allowing children to take jobs may improve financial status for the short term, but their lack of education jeopardizes their future economic well-being.

After taking an identity, a student uses the jobs, housing and transport files to make decisions. The market basket spreadsheet is used to calculate the weekly food and clothing budget. After entering this information, the spreadsheet is then activated by the student to calculate a weekly budget, a yearly budget and a 10-year projection. The student is encouraged to make changes in the initial selections and to observe the changes.

The exercise, however, is designed primarily to teach students to use the capabilities of Appleworks, the software developed for the Apple II computer. Included are working with different files, developing written material and saving it in a permanent file and using the spreadsheet to calculate changes in variables.

Unfortunately, directions on learning to use Appleworks are interspersed with making decisions about jobs, housing, clothing and food expenditures for an Irish immigrant family. This arrangement is somewhat confusing and also prevents the exercise from becoming a simulation.

The Irish Immigrant Experience is basically a problem-solving activity set in 1840. However, the data files developed for the program and the basic concept could form the nucleus of a well-designed simulation on managing the finances of a poor family in Boston in the 1840s.

The key issue in designing effective closed-structure simulations is to develop a challenging and absorbing exercise in which the available options and strategies are established in advance by the designer. In other words, the conceptual framework of the exercise should be developed in advance along with a map of the simulation similar to that developed for diagnostic simulations discussed in Chapter 4.

When the mathematical model and the decision points are selected, the exercise can be run informally in an open-structure format. Options and strategies undertaken by the students are noted and these selections become the options that are built into the computer program as the nucleus of the closed-structure exercise.

Variable-assignment exercises

In the early 1970s, several computer-based exercises were developed for the public school classroom that do not meet the criteria described for data-management simulations. In these exercises random events control the outcomes, the variables to which the participants assign values are superficial and relationships among the variables reflect an inadequate mathematical model. Two examples are *Lemonade Stand* and *Oregon Trail.*

Although purported to depend on logical decision-making, the exercises establish a Russian-roulette type of exercise in which the criteria for successful management are unknown to the participants. This type of computer-based exercise is referred to as a variable-assignment exercise for two reasons (Gredler, 1986). First, the student's only activity is that of repeatedly assigning values to a few variables identified in the computer program. Second, random events, other than the variables to which the participants have access, determine the outcomes of the exercise. Thus, participants do not hold the key to their own success; instead, they play against the odds established by the house (the computer). The student, like the gambler, rarely wins.

In addition to the dominance of random events, the selection of variables to which the students assign values is not based on a comprehensive model that is empirically based. As mentioned earlier, the exercise *Lemonade Stand* includes only three decisions: 1) the number of glasses of lemonade the students wish to sell; 2) the selling price per glass; and 3) the amount of money to be spent on advertising.

In *Lemonade Stand*, after the students input values for the three variables, the computer calculates the total expenditure, compares the calculations with a pre-programmed model and informs the students of the amount of profit or loss for that day. Sometimes this figure is accompanied by the statement that the weather was cloudy and rainy that day. Thus, little or no profit accrued to the lemonade stand operator. Another round then begins and the student makes the same decisions again with a subsequent evaluation by the computer program.

A review of computer software by Vargas (1986) states that the exercise 'omits such considerations as how much lemon and sugar to use per cup (the taste of the brew), where to locate the stand, how to calculate profit or loss, and the fact that few people would set up a stand on a rainy day' (p 742). Vargas notes that classifying the exercise as a simulation leads the prospective user to expect more than the exercise delivers.

A more serious flaw is found in *Oregon Trail* which purports to simulate the journey of a wagon train west to California. Specifically, the decisions the students are permitted to make have no influence on the outcome of the exercise. The students are asked to allocate a certain dollar amount of their funds to food, ammunition, clothing and miscellaneous supplies prior to undertaking the journey.

During the exercise, various events occur that deplete the students' resources. They are attacked by hostile riders, suffer broken legs, illnesses, broken wheels, blizzards (in August!) and these events are translated into changes in the dollar amount remaining in a particular category. As mentioned earlier in this chapter, the relationship between these random events and the money subtracted from the student's resources is arbitrary.

In addition, the only other reference to the journey is that the computer screen periodically illustrates a small graphics image of a wagon winding its way on a trail across the United States. Occasionally, students are permitted to choose to hunt or to fight hostile riders. At these points, the student presses a computer key to 'fire' shots at rabbits (food) or riders moving across the screen. This feature imitates events in video arcade games.

In summary, the exercise does not represent a journey west. The students do not experience the consequences of their decisions, and the exercise is based on a faulty mathematical model.

Open-structure simulations

Data-management simulations in the open-structure format are team exercises that are appropriate in a variety of subject areas, from political science to business. The typical paradigm in use is the allocation of resources to selected variables in a series of decision-making cycles or rounds. However, other paradigms should also be explored.

One paradigm that is underutilized in data-management simulations is for participants to construct their own database prior to the simulation. The constructed database is then used to make key decisions in the exercise.

An example is the open-structure simulation *On the Campaign Trail* (Fishel *et al.*, 1987). The election campaign for US senator takes place in the artificial state of Tarragon which is composed of 30 counties. Demographic and electoral data created for each county from the 1984 National Election Study include voter turnout and socio-economic status, race and media viewing habits of voters (Koch, 1991, p 120).

The class is divided into six groups with five students in each group. The six groups are randomly designated as three Democrat and three Republican and paired off for three separate senate campaigns (Koch, 1991, p 121). The Democratic candidate is Joe Clark and the Republican candidate is Chip Jones.

Prior to the simulation, the teams attend class lectures and complete assigned readings pertinent to the planning of a successful senate campaign. Each team then learns to calculate four measures important in planning a campaign. They are partisan strength, volatility of vote, percentage of the state-wide vote contributed by the candidate and voter turnout rate. Each team then classifies each county on these variables from the party's perspective. For example, on partisan strength, each county is classified as 'either a base county for the candidate, a competitive county or the opposition candidate's base county' (Koch, 1991, p 21).

In the simulation, teams first select the duration of the campaign, from one to ten weeks. The teams then allocate funds to televised spot ads, direct mail campaigns and surveys each week. The computer calculates the amount of money contributed to the candidate as a result of that week's expenditures. These results are analysed by the teams, compared to their developed database and the next week's campaign fund allocations are made.

In contrast, the majority of open-structure exercises are in business and they use the competitive game structure described earlier. The *Top Management Decision Simulation* developed in 1956 became the prototype for the exercises in use today. That is, several 'companies' are operating at the same time and are competing with each other. Feedback on team decisions is in the form of printouts from the computer which calculates the effects of the teams' decisions on particular variables in the exercises.

For the most part, developers of interactive business exercises have accepted company competiveness in terms of winners and losers as understood and they have concentrated on identifying surface structure elements. These elements include the number of cycles or rounds of decisions, initial financial position, resources to be manipulated and the rules for doing business, such as loan interest rates.

Designing business simulations that emphasize learning rather than winning, however, requires attention to deep structure issues. First, profit maximization as the goal should be replaced. Instead, simulations should emphasize only minimum profitability while positioning the company or institution for the long run (Teach, 1990).

Second, the teams should not manage the same type of institution in competition with each other. For example, three scenarios each with its associated mathematical model may be used simultaneously in the classroom. Each team's efforts in post-simulation sessions is reviewed in comparison to an optimal strategy for a particular institution or firm.

For example, some teams may be managing a small bank in a rural community and others may be managing a branch of an urban institution. Each team's task is to manage their institution in concert with the economic and social parameters of their region and the assets and disadvantages that are part of the institution's resources. In other words, some companies have lower labour costs and others have different advantages, such as location. The task of a manager is 'to do the most efficient job in the allocation of scarce resources to those uses that produce the most benefits for the firm' (Teach, 1990, p 19).

Third, establishing an environment in which team members can experience reality of function is enhanced if each team member is assigned a viable role as a department or division head *with associated decision-making responsibility*. If the simulation involves a bank, for instance, one person may be in charge of short-term loans, another may be responsible for long-term loans and another is responsible for customer savings. Their goals for their areas of responsibility must be balanced against the goals they establish for the institution.

Fourth, the stimuli that precipitate participant actions should not be restricted to computer printouts received at the beginning of each cycle. Instead, like the other tactical-decision simulations, peripheral roles that are meaningful in the particular exercise may be taken by project staff, interim reports on the institution's operations may be requested by the bank's president and so on.

Finally, data-management simulations, particularly in the 'information age' brought about in part by computers, can fulfil an important role in several subject areas. However, the conceptual models for such simulations must be as carefully thought through as the mathematical models that establish the empirical relationships among the variables.

EVALUATING DATA-MANAGEMENT SIMULATIONS

Step 1: Review the empirical model for the simulation.
- Is the model comprehensive (ie, it is not a linear relationship restricted to two or three variables)?
- Are the relationships among the variables arbitrary or do they reflect generalizable rules?
- Is the empirical model dominated by random events (a variable-assignment exercise) or are consequences the result of participant decisions?
- Are quantifiable variables the basis for the model or are qualitative relationships inaccurately assigned a numerical value?
- Is the empirical model explained in the instructor's materials?
- Is the model resilient to extreme decisions that may be made by participants?

Step 2: Evaluate the conceptual model.
- Does the exercise avoid categorizing participants as winners or losers?
- Is participant decision-making permitted across a variety of categories?
- Is the exercise a data-management simulation or is it an

exercise that requires simply tapping into a particular data set?

- Does the model depend on repetitive decision-making in a series of cycles?

Step 3: Determine the potential of the exercise for providing reality of function for the participants.

- Are the designated roles viable and clearly associated with a specific responsibility?
- Is participant action initiated in response to more than one type of stimulus or event?
- Do the participants experience meaningful consequences as a result of their decisions?
- Do the participants control the direction of the exercise by the types of decisions they make?

REFERENCES

Adams, F G and Geczy, C C (1991) 'International economic policy simulation games on the microcomputer', *Social Science Computer Review*, **9**, 2, 191–201.

Carlson, P (1969) *Learning Through Games*, Washington, DC: Public Affairs Press.

Faria, A J (1987) 'A survey of the use of business games in academia and business', *Simulation and Games 18*, 207–24.

Fishel, M, Gopoion, D and Stacey, J (1987) *On the Campaign Trail*, Washington DC: Campaigns and Elections.

Fisher, G (1982) 'Lemonade stand (and other simulations) for sale', *Electronic Learning*, February, 78–82.

Galitz, L C (1983) '*Interbank:* A bank management simulation exercise', *Journal of Banking and Finance*, **7**, 355–82.

Ginter, P M and Rucks, A C (1983) 'War games and business strategy formulation', *Managerial Planning*, **32**, 2, 15–34.

Golden, P A and Smith, J R (1991) 'A simulation director's perspective', *Simulation and Gaming*, 1, 84–5.

Gredler, M (1986) 'A taxonomy of microcomputer simulations', *Educational Technology*, **22**, 4, 7–12.

Koch, N S (1991) 'The pedagogical value of political science microcomputer simulations: An evaluation of *On The Campaign Trail*, *Social Science Computer Review*, **9**, 1, 119–23.

Lundy, J (1985) 'The effects of competition in business games' in van Ments, M and Hearnden, K (eds), *Effective Use of Games and Simulation*, 199–208, Loughborough University: SAGSET.

Tansey, P and Unwin, D (1969) *Simulation and Gaming in Education*, London: Methuen.

Teach, R D (1990) 'Profits: The false prophet in business gaming', *Simulation and Gaming*, **21**, 1, 12–16.

Vargas, J S (1986) 'Instructional design flaws in computer-assisted instruction', *Phi Delta Kappan*, **64**, 738–44.

Wing, R (1968) 'Two computer-based economic games for sixth graders', in Boocock, S and Schild E (eds), *Simulation Games in Learning*, 155–65, Beverly Hills, CA: Sage.

8 Social-system simulations

Tactical-decision simulations are a group of exercises in which the focus is that of participants interacting with explicit problems or crises. The primary intent is that of developing participants' cognitive strategies, ie, their capabilities of data selection, organization, interpretation and management.

In contrast, social-process simulations are those exercises that focus on interactions among people and the ways that one's beliefs, assumptions, goals and actions may be hindered or assisted in interactions with others. Included in this group are social-system, language skills/communication and empathy/insight simulations.

The foundation of social-system simulations is the complex supporting fabric of relations found in organized groups. Human beings, unlike other species that live in groups, have developed multifaceted systems of social life. Depending on the particular community and its culture, one's actions may lead to any of a variety of consequences, based on the shared (often unstated) understandings that guide daily affairs. Ethnographers spend months and even years in cultures different from their own to discover the often complex web of beliefs and practices that support the particular social organization they seek to understand. Social-system simulations provide participants with the opportunity to discover some of the beliefs and practices that support social life in their own or another culture.

OVERVIEW

Social-system simulations are appropriate in a variety of subject areas and at all educational levels. They are used when experiencing a particular cultural process or processes is the goal.

Early developments

The grandparent of social-system simulations is the international relations simulation developed by Harold Guetzkow, Northwestern University and Cleo Cherryholmes, Michigan State University. Developed in the late 1950s, the exercise, *Inter-nation Simulation*, was originally developed for research into behavioural patterns among nations. That is, it was a hypothetical model of nations functioning in an international system.

Participants functioned as representatives of five to seven hypothetical nations (eg, Algo, Enge), members of the International Organization and the producers of the World Newspaper. Each nation's representatives included a head of state, a foreign policy advisor, an official domestic advisor, a foreign affairs diplomat and the domestic opposition leader.

Prior to the exercise, the representatives of each country received key information about their nation. Included were type of government, types of resources, status of wealth, population and a statistical report on consumer satisfaction, national security, the probability of revolution and other factors.

In each 70-minute cycle (which equalled one year), each decision-maker attempted to achieve the goals he or she had established for the nation. Military alliances, trade agreements, economic treaties and other activities were permitted. At the beginning of each cycle, participants also received a copy of the World Newspaper which summarized the important events of the previous cycle as well as some secret messages that had been intercepted.

One feature of *Inter-nation Simulation* that resembles some data-management simulations is the computer analyses of participant decisions at the end of each cycle. Mathematical equations developed in the original analyses of international processes were used to calculate new indices for the start of the next cycle on a variety of variables, such as citizen satisfaction and the nation's status (Guetzkow and Valdez, 1981; Guetzkow *et al.*, 1963).

Communications between nations were either by visit or written. However, written communications and requests for conferences or visits were routed through the nation's external decision-makers. If the internal decision-makers did not organize themselves adequately, they became bogged down in events. Also, rapidly occurring external events made communication difficult between external and internal decision-makers. In summary, decision-makers were constantly faced with diverse events within their broad areas of responsibility, illustrating the difficulty of mediating on several fronts simultaneously.

Other early developments that followed *Inter-nation Simulation* also attempted to model complete social systems. However, the perspective that a major design goal is to model a social *system* resulted in complex exercises that sometimes made use of artificial actions by participants. An example is *SIMSOC* in which a society is divided into four regions (blue, green, yellow and red) with striking differences in their allocated resources (Gamson, 1978). The task for participants is to establish a society in a situation characterized by extreme regional inequality, no group structure, no consensus on individual goals, lack of government and lack of a legitimate basis for privilege (Dukes, 1980, p 251).

The principal means of taking action in *SIMSOC*, however, is by filling out forms. In addition to individual goal declaration forms, 14 other forms are used (A to O). Participants work, move, enjoy luxuries, support political parties, join various groups, subscribe to the media and riot or repress by completing forms (Dukes, 1980, p 256). Although the forms provide evidence that an event has taken place, use of this mechanism sacrifices spontaneity. Also, the exercise includes an 180-page manual of rules and solutions to unanticipated problems.

Major characteristics

In tactical-decision simulations, participants face a complex problem or crisis and their interactions with that situation propel the simulation. In contrast, participants in social-system simulations face a decision-making event that requires interactions among the participants and it is these interactions that propel the simulation.

The primary purpose of social-system simulations is for participants to experience some of the dynamic social and/or political processes that are part of the fabric of organized social groups. Participants are attempting to fulfil any of a range of social and/or political goals that depend on interaction with others. Examples range from organizing others against increased use of nuclear power to attempting to become assimilated into a strange culture. Strategies that may emerge during a simulation include cooperation, negotiation, persuasion, confrontation and others.

The components of a social-system simulation that are developed by the designer are a) a precipitating event; b) complicating factors; c) participant roles; and d) context. All of these components interact with each other to set in motion the interactions among participants that are the core of the simulation.

For example, the precipitating event may be a proposed nuclear energy plant in a poor coastal area considered to be an environmental refuge for several species of birds. Residents of the area hold different views on the impact of the plant on jobs and the environment according to their position in the community and other characteristics (roles). A complicating factor is that many of the area's residents are unemployed poor farmers for whom the plant may offer jobs. The setting is a town meeting in which the villagers air the issues prior to a vote.

Social-system simulations are similar to the other social-process simulations in at least two ways. First, the participants typically experience emotional reactions, from confusion and frustration, to a sense of pride, disappointment or perhaps even anger. Therefore, an essential facet of the experience is the post-simulation session in which emotions are addressed, contributing factors are explored and relationships to analogous situations may be proposed by the participants and explored. Second (unlike tactical-decision simulations), events and outcomes depend for the most part on the interpersonal dynamics that evolve as the simulation progresses.

Sub-types

Two different sub-types of social-system simulations are multi-agenda and single-agenda exercises. In multi-agenda simulations, participants assume individual roles with different perspectives and/or priorities. They experience the effects of attempting to meet their particular goals or to address an issue in a context in which other voices and views also seek verification and fulfilment. The dynamics of the simulation unfold as the roles are executed by the participants. *Inter-nation Simulation* is one example of this type.

In contrast, the single-agenda simulation establishes a situation in which participants experience the effects of a particular process or mechanism. In this type of exercise, specific individual roles are not assigned. Instead, each participant is simply one of several in a designated group and the group experiences the effects of a particular social process or mechanism.

An example is *Talking Rocks*. Participants are prehistoric shepherds known as the Eagle people. They live in groups and migrate with the seasons. Each group of Eagle people is placed at a 'camp site' in the room or in two separate rooms, if possible. The groups move simultaneously from one camp site to another.

During the migrations, each group must leave a survival message for the others on a large easel placed at each site. However, the survival messages (written in English for the group) must be left in picture form. Contemporary signs and symbols, such as '+' or '=' and numbers may not be used.

When each group arrives at a new camp site, their task is to decipher the message left for them and to leave their own message. Only the groups that successfully decipher the messages from the others survive. Of interest is that survival often is based on receiving a good message that is fairly easy to decipher, whereas death may result from receiving an unclear message (Jones, 1982).

Talking Rocks challenges the stereotypical idea that primitive people were unsophisticated. In other words, ingenuity and talent are required to leave messages for others in the absence of a written language system.

Inappropriate uses of technology

Among the products developed by commercial companies are 'simulations' that attempt to deliver a social experience by computer. Such exercises typically require decision-making by students in a social or political context and the computer 'reports' the reactions of others who are affected in some way by these decisions.

One such exercise developed for the Apple computer requires that the class first be divided into teams. Each team takes the position of the leader of a hypothetical country, Libros. After reading a brief scenario, each team rank orders its priorities across four choices (eg, get re-elected, protect Libran citizens in the neighbouring threatened country and so on).

Each team then enters its priorities into the computer and is presented with three options from which to select a course of action. However, prior to making a choice, the computer screen displays four faces of selected 'advisors'. Each face is numbered and carries a label that represents a particular policy, such as 'domino effect'.

At this point, the students are to consult a booklet that accompanies the exercise for the paragraph under 'domino effect'. Theoretically, each of the four 'advisors' is to be consulted in this way. The team then selects a course of action from the three policy choices presented earlier. This scenario continues through other decision points in the same manner. At the conclusion of the exercise, the program reports the number of points earned by each team according to the extent to which they fulfilled their priorities.

Teachers who were evaluating this exercise after running it several times were unable to conclude with a peaceful resolution. Continued hostilities and escalation of war preparations occurred on each run.

Several surface structure problems are present in this exercise. First, stopping the exercise to consult booklets is not practical. Second, a team may make a policy decision without consulting the advisors. Third, assigning points to foreign policy decisions introduces inappropriate game elements as does the team competition. Fourth, the options from which one may make a selection are simplistic and frustrating.

The deep structure problems with the exercise are that it trivializes a complex and subtle issue and presents a distorted version of a complex interactive experience. Further, some of the 'advice' paragraphs are not applicable to the particular situation and may be misunderstood and distorted by the students. For example, the American intervention policy in Korea is reported as one type of solution. The context surrounding that decision is unlikely to be analogous to a fictitious situation with few identified parameters.

Finally, interaction with a computer program when the goal of the exercise is that of experiencing a complex social process sends undesirable curriculum messages. Among them are that choices in international problems are limited to a few unilateral alternatives and that it is impossible to resolve an international situation and remain true to one's established priorities.

MAJOR DESIGN ISSUES

Key issues in the design of a social-system simulation are establishing the context or framework for participant interactions and the mechanisms to be used for ensuring the social exchanges.

Establishing the context

Two approaches to designing the simulation framework have been used by developers. One is that of first modelling the social system and then attempting to fit a simulation to the model. The second approach emphasizes instead the primary experiences and processes that participants are to undergo during the simulation.

Modelling the social system

Implementing this approach requires setting objectives for the simulation and then developing a conceptual model of the system that is to be simulated. Further, the model that is developed is often illustrated schematically. A conceptual model of a poor Third World village, for example, might include a list of villagers illustrating goals, activities and resources; a schematic illustrating the ways that farmers allocate their time and capital; and a schematic of factors that contribute to losses in the farmers' productive time.

The development of a conceptual model of a social system as an initial step in design is based on the assumption that the goal is to simulate the system. However, several problems arise from this perspective. First, the correspondence between the model and the real-world setting is often based on the designer's unexamined common sense preconceptions of the setting (Sharrock and Watson, 1987, p 39). Thus, events in the simulation will be distorted events of some real-world system.

Second, recreating all the elements in a social system is an overwhelming task. Third, it is likely to result in a complicated exercise for both participants and directors. Fourth, the result is that the surface characteristics of a system may be replicated, but the essence of the experience of being a member of the system may be lost.

Fifth, modelling the social system sets up some participants to be winners and others to be losers. That is, the losers

> are such not by lower ability or less effort, but because we have deliberately given them unequal resources to win because their real-world counterparts have unequal resources ... we have created conditions of failure in some groups and generated feelings of failure in attaining group goals (Greenblat, 1980, p 45).

One participant in *The Green Revolution Game*, referred to as an excellent reproduction of village life in India, nevertheless describes his feelings during the exercise:

> Pangs of jealousy arose in me when it became clear that one 'family' had lots of land, relatively few children, and enough money to irrigate their land, try new seed varieties, and borrow substantial sums from the town money lender. I struggled [and] not having credit enough to suit the money-lender, I had to visit the rich family to borrow cash, a humiliating experience (Getis, 1984, p 119).

Finally, modelling the social system locks in the designer to two specific problems that seriously threaten reality of function for the participants. One is that efforts to imitate the range of events that occurs in the 'society' lead to artificial events or illustrations. For example, in the *Community Land Use Game (CLUG)*, players buy and sell land parcels that are portrayed on a game board. Despite decisions such as locating utility pipes, constructing commercial enterprises and paying taxes, the use of 'cash' for transactions and the board orientation lead some participants to comment on the similarity to *Monopoly* (Davis, 1980).

The second threat to reality of function is that simulating a society involves developing a variety of roles that appear in the social system, but which may not be equally important in contributing to participant experiences in the exercise. An example is a simulation intended to address the situation of individuals fighting a debilitating disease while attempting to function in society. Modelling the social system as a basis for the exercise requires including patients, family members, employers, doctors and other health-care workers, as well as representatives from the insurance and welfare systems. The result is the inclusion of some roles that are not functional for the role-takers. That is, the roles may fuel the experience of others, but may be less than satisfactory for the participants who take them.

Identifying key processes

A well-known characteristic of simulations is that one cannot specify in advance the particular thoughts, emotions and attitudes that individuals will experience as a result of participating in the exercise. However, designers can identify the key *processes* that participants are to experience *during* the simulation. That is, social-system simulations may involve participants in one or two general situations. Specifically, the participants may a) encounter events precipitated by different perspectives on an issue, task or policy or b) undergo a particular social process or mechanism that challenges their particular assumptions or expectations about society.

St Philip is an example of a social-process simulation in which events are precipitated by different perspectives on an issue. Participants take roles as hotel developers and members of the parliament of the Caribbean island, St Philip. The MPs hold different perspectives on the effects of a proposed hotel development for the island that is intended to promote tourism.

The goal of encountering different perspectives indicates that a multi-agenda simulation should be designed. In a multi-agenda simulation, the different roles taken by participants, each with a responsibility related to the precipitating event, and the associated factors are the nucleus of the simulation.

In contrast, if the experience is that of undergoing events that challenge one's assumptions and beliefs about some aspect of social functioning, then a single-agenda simulation is indicated. Participants do not take individual roles in such exercises. Instead, they are placed in a situation (precipitating event) in which their typical actions are initially ineffective and their beliefs are challenged. An example touched on earlier is *Talking Rocks* (described by Jones (1982)), in which participants are members of a prehistoric nomadic tribe that lacks a written symbol system. Small groups in their 'travels' must leave key survival information for the others without using written symbols. This simulation challenges the typical belief that prehistoric people lacked creativity and ingenuity.

Sometimes the expectation is that participation in *any* social-process simulation will lead to a rethinking of one's assumptions and beliefs. However, multi-agenda simulations only provide opportunities for participants with different perspectives to interact. The direction that events will take depends in large measure on the actions of others. Thus, the behavioural contingencies that guarantee ineffective action by participants (which establishes the climate for rethinking) are not necessarily present.

Identification of the key processes that are to be set in motion by the simulation identifies the type: single or multi-agenda. Any of a variety of different situations may be constructed in either format.

Note that the key processes are not described in terms of a particular situation, society, group or subject area. Too early an emphasis on subject area or content complicates the design process and may result in a simulation that does not provide the desired experiences. An example is stating that participants are to experience the complexity of urban issues and the effects of coalition building. First, the designer cannot prescribe that one 'experience complexity'. The designer can only establish a situation in which conflicts and misunderstandings arise over subtle points.

Second, 'urban issues' locks the designer *a priori* into a particular context which may inadvertently focus the developer's attention on the identification of content-related items instead of the key aspects of the experience for the participants. Third, experiencing the *effects* of coalition building also is unclear.

Multi-agenda simulations

In multi-agenda simulations, participants seek to fulfil certain goals or to establish particular priorities in a context in which a variety of views and priorities may be operating. The simulation can take any of a variety of directions, depending on the parameters established by the designer.

The general direction taken in a simulation is determined in large measure by the nature of the precipitating event or issue, the complicating and facilitating factors introduced by the designer, the roles of the participants and the context.

The precipitating event is a situation with both positive and negative features. The determination of which are more important depends on the perspective provided in the role description of each participant. In *St Philip* (Walford, 1983) the precipitating event is a proposed hotel development for tourists on St Philip, a poor Caribbean island. However, the livelihood of the poor banana farmers is likely to be threatened. Further, tourists have no access to the island; therefore, an airstrip must be built (complicating factors).

Participants take roles as hotel developers and members of the island's parliament from different political parties with different views on the proposal. The context is a day in parliament in which informal meetings are followed by a formal session and a vote.

During the simulation, various issues both pro and con are raised as participants attempt to convince their colleagues of the worth of their particular stand. In contrast, a different climate is established by introducing other elements into the basic components. For example, cooperation and compromise may be introduced by altering the role cards to indicate a basis for negotiation. Specifically, a constituency opposes the development unless certain guarantees are provided, such as taxes paid by the hotel developer. These taxes are to be used for advanced education of the islanders in professions such as health care, teaching and law. The need for an airstrip (complicating factor) may be changed to an undeveloped marina with one constituency interested in providing a port in which commercial cargo ships can efficiently transport the island's banana crop to market. These changes establish the climate for the different perspectives to hammer out a compromise.

Interaction of components

Well-designed simulations do not depend on complex sets of rules or gaming elements such as earning points or exchanging chips. Instead, involved interactions by the participants result from the interface of the major components. In other words, roles are chosen that will have a vested interest in the outcome of the precipitating event. For example, businessmen, artists, senior citizens and teachers have a vested interest in the ways that a surplus in a city's budget is to be spent.

Careful consideration of the relationships between the precipitating event, selected roles and the context provides several benefits. First, as already mentioned, is the avoidance of complex sets of rules. Second, the factors that stimulate specific participant actions are spread among the individual cards. Thus, each participant has an assigned responsibility or goal to achieve and a reason to interact with others. Finally, a minimum amount of background information is needed for the participants.

Roles
Several recommendations are important in the selection and development of participant roles. First, all roles should have a stake in the outcome of the exercise. Therefore, the number of participants should be no larger than the number that can interact with each other throughout the simulation. Depending on the situation, this number may vary from 5 to about 12. Occasionally, a developer will recommend that a larger number of participants may be accommodated than the number of roles originally specified by adding assistants or secretaries to key decision-makers. The disadvantage of this mechanism is that the additional roles do not interact with the precipitating event and other key roles in the same way as the primary decision-makers.

Second, it is important that the roles should be ones to which the participants can commit their thoughts and feelings. One should not expect, for example, a middle-class white student to take the role of a poor, inner-city minority student whose family is homeless. If the purpose of the simulation is for the participant to experience the frustrations, anger and other emotions of an inner-city homeless person, then a different kind of simulation is needed (see Chapter 10).

Third, the relationship of the particular role to the precipitating event is the primary means of establishing credibility of the role. Each role card should specify a position, priority or question to be addressed and sufficient supporting information for the participant to act. Thus, the role card should be brief – one paragraph is recommended.

Role cards for the members of parliament in St Philip describe the source of the individual's livelihood (eg, small hotel owner, a banana-farm foreman), one's constituency (eg, poor banana-farm workers, citizens of Queenstown) and other relevant information on one's position. Brian Samuel, for example, is the MP for Mid-Island and is also minister of education. He is concerned about preserving the island's tradition and is suspicious of development that may change things too fast (Walford, 1983, p 173). In contrast, the question for Evelyn Talbot, an ex-colonial sugar planter, is whom she needs to convince to support the new development.

Fourth, artefacts and gaming elements should not be used to 'prime' participants' actions. For example, in one exercise a role card specifies that a student's task is to escape the teacher's attention by daydreaming, which is defined as drawing six-pointed stars. The role card also specifies that the student will receive one point for each star, five points each time another student smiles at him or her and five points when the teacher smiles at the student. Such a mechanism, however, focuses the participant's attention on earning points. Instead, if a particular behaviour is important in the simulation, it should be stimulated by the precipitating event, the actions of others or the direction that the simulation is taking at a particular moment.

Single-agenda simulations

The purpose of a single-agenda simulation is for participants to experience the effects of a particular mechanism or process that challenges their expectations. The essence of the single-agenda simulation is to place participants in a situation in which their customary actions are ineffective. Participants, in order to be successful, must rethink their actions. In *Talking Rocks*, for example, participants must devise new methods of communication.

The Crisis Game, described in Chapter 6, is another example. The purpose is for participants to experience the tension and time pressure that can accompany foreign-policy decision-making. Participants are divided into teams to develop recommendations on a current issue in a limited amount of time. They are then subjected to unexpected interruptions and to a decrease in the time allowed to complete their work. The precipitating event is the administration's need for a policy document and the complicating factors are the periodic announcements of other information and the further limitation of the time to complete the task.

Ideally, the single-agenda simulation should be as free as possible of artificial rules and paraphernalia. The greater the reliance on contrived circumstances or artefacts, the more that reality of function for the participant is threatened.

An example of a simple yet effective single-agenda simulation is *The Numbers Game*. The class is divided into teams and each team receives a set of cards. Each card has one equation in a set of simultaneous equations, such as 'A + D = 4', 'B + E – C = 2' and so on. The task for each team is to determine the value of D (Jaques, 1981).

Typically, participants begin to ask questions, such as 'Are we to do this as a team?', 'Are we competing with the other teams?', 'What are we supposed to do?' (Jaques, 1981). Because the instructor does not answer the questions, the teams are forced to deal with the ambiguity of the situation and settle down to the task. Often, when the first team shouts out an answer, the other teams become agitated. (However, each team has a different set of equations.)

The exercise reveals the assumptions that are made in common social settings, in particular, the classroom. They are that 'competition is valued above cooperation; there is a single right answer to every question; and authority will guide you if you are uncertain about where to go' (Jaques, 1981, p 150). However, the exercise also reveals that cooperation leads to the most effective team functioning, and the established problem is the only one that is to be solved (Jaques, 1981).

This exercise is particularly appropriate in a classroom that is about to undertake a two- to four-week restructuring and to make use of cooperative learning (see DeVries and Edwards, 1973, and Slavin, 1980, for descriptions of cooperative learning structures). This particular exercise reveals basic assumptions as well as providing a mechanism for preparing for the revised classroom structure.

A well-known example of a single-agenda simulation is *BaFa BaFa*. Participants become members of either the Alpha or Beta culture, each of which has different social rules. The Alpha culture is affectionate and friendly, engaging frequently in hugging, patting shoulders and standing close to each other during conversations. The culture is also patriarchal and does not permit women to approach a male to begin a conversation. In addition, each conversation begins by discussing the accomplishments of male relatives.

Although the Alphans, after initial conversation with each other, engage in a card-matching game that results in the exchange of chips, it is far more important to have fun than to win chips. Alphans also sign each other's Alpha membership cards when they part company if they believe the other has obeyed the rules of the culture.

In contrast, in the Beta culture, one acquires worth by becoming an effective trader. This goal requires hard bargaining and persistence. Successful bargaining for numbered cards of different colours requires the use of a special language code that combines vowels with consonants in particular ways. Using fingers or counting in other ways is not permitted during bargaining.

The situation is designed so that visitors from the other culture will only have a few minutes to attempt to adjust to a culture with diametrically opposed values. Thus, the trading-oriented Betas, for example, will insult the Alphans by initiating conversations with women and appearing greedy at card playing. In contrast, Alphans will appear inept to the Betans as well as failing to value the 'right' priorities.

Post-simulation analysis has typically revealed that the alien culture is described in less than complimentary terms. Betans are seen as 'cold' and 'greedy' whereas Alphans are often felt to be 'lazy' and 'naive'. In other words, attempting to become a member of another culture is initially accompanied by embarrassment, frustration and a sense of strangeness (Shirts, 1977).

Participants who work at becoming Alphas or Betas can experience the intended effects when visiting the other culture. However, becoming familiar with one's assigned culture can be a wearing experience as one practises the prescribed rituals and attempts to make appropriate use of cards and symbols. Also, participants spend the maximum amount of time working at being an Alphan or Betan with a disproportionately short time experiencing the difficulties of cultural transfer. Some participants tend to lose interest before their visit to the other culture.

Both single-agenda and multi-agenda simulations can provide a window on human social life in which the participants interact with each other in a variety of ways. An important component in the learning, however, is the types of post-simulation activities that build on the interactive experience. These activities are discussed in Chapter 11.

EVALUATING SOCIAL-SYSTEM SIMULATIONS

Step 1: Determine the sub-type (single or multi-agenda).
- Are roles assigned to individuals or do participants function as a group?
- Do the participants undergo a particular social process or do they encounter events precipitated by the different roles?

Multi-agenda simulations

Step 2: Analyse the precipitating event and context.
- Does the event have both positive and negative features?
- Is the task related to the precipitating event clear and unambiguous for the participants?
- Is the precipitating event credible for the selected context?
- Are the complicating factors credible?
- Are the rules simple and easy to learn?

Step 3: Review participant roles.
- Is each role active and essential?
- Does each role card specify a position, priority or question to be addressed and sufficient supporting information for action?
- Do the roles reflect a range of credible perspectives?
- Can the simulation take any of a variety of directions, given the roles?
- Are the roles free of artificial mechanisms?

Single-agenda simulations

Step 2: Analyse the social situation that initiates the simulation.

- What are the accepted assumptions that the situation challenges?
- Is the situation credible?
- Is the situation easy to establish and free of complex rules?

Step 3: Review the group role.

- Is the task for the group(s) clear and easily understood?
- What are the complications in the situation that interact with the task (eg, the Eagle people cannot use contemporary symbols; time pressures increase in *The Crisis Game*)?
- Is the group task free of artificial elements and complex rules?
- What behavioural changes are likely to occur during the situation?

REFERENCES

Davis, J L (1980) 'Community Land Use Game: An Evaluation', in Horn, R E and Cleaves, A (eds), *The Guide to Simulations/Games for Education and Training* (4th edn), 45–50, Beverly Hills, CA: Sage.

DeVries, D and Edwards, K (1973) 'Learning games and student teams: Their effects on classroom process', *American Educational Research Journal*, **10**, 307–18.

Dukes, R A (1980) 'SIMSOC: An Evaluation', in Horn, R E and Cleaves, A (eds) *The Guide to Simulations/Games for Education and Training* (4th edn), 248–61, Beverly Hills, CA: Sage.

Gamson, W A (1978) *SIMSOC, Simulated Society: Coordinator's Manual*, New York: Free Press.

Getis, A (1984) 'Game review: The Green Revolution Game', *Simulation and Games*, **15**, 1, 119–20.

Greenblat, C (1980) 'Group dynamics and game design', *Simulation and Games*, **11**, 1, 35–58.

Guetzkow, H and Valdez: J J (1981) 'International relations theory: Contributions of simulated international processes', in Guetzkow, H and Valdez, J J (eds) *Simulated International Processes: Theory and Research in Global Modeling*, Beverly Hills, CA: Sage.

Guetzkow, H, Alger, C F, Brody, R A, Noel, R C and Snyder, R C (1963) *Simulation in International Relations: Developments for Research and Teaching*, Englewood Cliffs, NJ: Prentice-Hall.

Jaques, D (1981) 'Games for all seasons', *Simulation/Games for Learning*, **11**, 4, 147–56.

Jones, K (1982) *Simulations in Language Teaching*, Cambridge: Cambridge University Press.

Sharrock, W W and Watson, D R (1987) ' "Power" and "realism" in simulation and gaming: Some pedagogic and analytic observations', 35–41, in Crookall, D *et al.* (eds) *Simulation-gaming in the late 1980s*, Oxford: Pergamon.

Shirts, R G (1977) *BaFa BaFa*, La Jolla, CA: Simile II

Slavin, R E (1980) 'Cooperative learning', *Review of Educational Research*, **50**, 2, 315–42.

Talking Rocks, La Jolla, CA: Simile II.

Walford, R (1983) St Philip: A simulation about the development of a Caribbean Island', *Journal of Geography*, July–August, 170–75.

9 Language skills/communication simulations

Social-process simulations, by their very nature, involve participants in communication. Resolving an issue such as tourism in *St Philip*, for example, requires orally presenting one's views cogently, as well as persuasion, mediation and negotiation. In contrast, participants in *The Numbers Game*, finding themselves in an uncertain situation, begin by using language to seek information.

Simulations selected for some aspect of language or communication skills development may be chosen for any of a variety of reasons. Among them are to provide students learning English with practice in concrete situations, to develop students' interviewing, writing, and/or listening skills, and to analyse later the flow of discourse and how it developed.

OVERVIEW

In recent years, simulations have become an important activity in language learning. Currently, the purposes of implementing simulations in the language classroom and the role of technology are important issues.

Prior developments

Simulations for language skills and communication are applicable in a variety of areas. In language teaching, their use is a relatively new development. It is an outgrowth of the 'communicative' movement of the 1970s that altered the focus of language teaching (K Jones, 1982). The direction changed to that of developing students' skills and strategies for communicating effectively in concrete situations.

Another use is in medical education. Medical schools use simulated patients both to teach and to assess students' interviewing skills (eg, Hanney, 1980; McAvoy, 1988). The 'patient' is provided with a description of his or her family situation, medical background and current symptoms. He or she then responds to the questions of the medical student who takes the role of the patient's doctor. Individuals who take the roles of patients may be faculty, actors or advanced students in other fields.

Three advantages of simulated patients are a) availability at a particular time and place; b) the avoidance of trauma to the individual with a terminal illness when interviewed by an inexperienced student; and c) replication. That is, the same 'patient' may be interviewed by four or five students, thus providing a standardized situation when the interviews are used for assessment.

In most situations, the interviews are videotaped for later analysis. Some schools evaluate the interviews for both information-seeking and empathy. In addition, the 'patient' provides personal feedback to the supervisor and the student.

One study compared student interviews of real and simulated patients (Sanson-Fisher and Poole, 1980). No differences in empathy were found by assessors who had no knowledge of the nature of the study. No significant differences were found for 40 students who each interviewed one bona fide and one simulated patient. Moreover, the students were unable to discriminate between the two groups.

At present, Southern Illinois University uses the medical examination and interviewing of simulated patients as part of the clinical final examination. Also, the American Medical Association is considering the use of patient interviewing in licensing examinations for doctors.

Purposes

The goal of simulations for language skills and communication is to help develop abilities to think and communicate in unfamiliar situations (K Jones, 1982, p 9). Several advantages of simulations over other activities, such as classroom discussions, have been identified. First, simulations expand the range and variety of communication situations with which students interact. The dominant model of language in the classroom is teacher talk (Scarcella and Crookall, 1990). As a result, students may not have sufficient exposure to other forms of communication, such as participating in a casual conversation among friends or addressing a misunderstanding in the work setting. Simulations can expose students to a variety of language experiences that include apologies, promises, compliments and other types of expression.

Second, simulations change the role of teachers and learners and encourage students to take a more responsible role in the learning process (Oxford and Crookall, 1990). Students also have the opportunity to be creative in their use of language instead of responding to 'test' questions posed by the teacher.

Third, simulations can tap a variety of communication skills (K Jones, 1982). For example, a simple exercise is that of planning a trip to another planet to form a new civilisation (Scarcella and Stern, 1990, p 121). Participants receive background information about life on other planets and each group selects their new home. Because storage is limited on the spaceship, participants must decide which items from earth should be transported with them. Skills tapped in such an exercise include reading, brainstorming, negotiation and writing.

Fourth, simulations expand the number and type of interesting situations that may be used (K Jones, 1982). Included are imaginative simulations, such as *Space Crash* and social situations that are new to the student, such as planning a week's programme for the Arts Centre.

Perhaps most important is that the activity in a simulation is voluntary and spontaneous as is the use of language in everyday communication (K Jones, 1982, p 11). The participants communicate and confer with each other as they develop and execute the mechanisms to accomplish their goals in their duties as committee members, diplomats or interplanetary visitors. Participants in *Space Crash*, for example, share vital information in order to survive on a strange planet. In *Radio Covingham*, participants develop and broadcast a 'news and comments' radio programme.

Two general purposes may be identified for the use of language skills simulations. They are 1) to provide students with opportunities to stretch their communicative skills and 2) to provide data for the diagnosis and analysis of language errors. The latter is undertaken by the teacher in order to identify problems or issues to be addressed in subsequent lessons.

Any tabulation of errors, however, should be conducted unobtrusively and should not be used to determine scores or grades for individual students. Otherwise, the spontaneity of the participants' language use and their efforts to push their capabilities to meet new challenges will be seriously jeopardized. Therefore, although the two purposes are not mutually exclusive, they must be executed with care when used in tandem.

Major characteristics

Simulations for communication skills are not restricted to language classrooms. Instead, they are appropriate for a variety of learning situations. A simulation in which success depends on the accurate exchange of information, for example, is appropriate for students learning English, the social studies classroom, the corporate boardroom and others.

Simulations selected for communication skills need not be developed expressly for that purpose. For example, the single-agenda simulation, *The Crisis Game*, described in Chapter 8, is also appropriate for language learning situations.

Four characteristics of simulations used for language skills are essential. One is that the simulation should establish a compelling situation that completely absorbs the attention and actions of the participants. The importance of this characteristic is that participants will be less self-conscious about their language use.

Interest in *Radio Covingham*, for instance, is maintained in several ways. First the simulation establishes the need to conduct interviews and to develop interesting commentaries from the interviews. Second is the arrival of additional news items until broadcast time. Third, the participants work under two kinds of time limitations – one being the amount of time allowed for producing the programme, the other, that of making the broadcast fit the 10-minute time allocation.

Space Crash, in contrast, provides a life-threatening situation for the space crew. Each of the five role cards for the crew members describes some of the information essential to finding food and water and thereby surviving on a strange planet. The simulation begins with one map card which is placed in the centre of the table. The card shows a crashed spacecraft and is labelled 'flatland'. Once the crew has decided which way to go, they may request another map square from the director. Then they may request subsequent squares, one at a time as they determine their route across the planet (K Jones, 1982).

The second essential characteristic is that the situation must be language-intensive for each participant. That is, participants cannot assume passive roles. For example, simulations in which two or more teams are established with three or four members per team can provide opportunities for one or two members to dominate the discussion. However, this problem can be mitigated somewhat by providing some item of key information on each role card.

Third, the situation established for the simulation should be one that can go in any of a variety of directions, depending on the approaches taken by the participants. Such a situation increases interest because the participants essentially mould events within the given framework. In *Radio Covingham*, for instance, participants are provided with listeners' letters that arrived in the morning post, the station manager's memo and handouts. The participants' first task is to decide on the general outline for the broadcast. That is, should all the news be presented first or scattered throughout the broadcast and should special segments be included on particular subjects, such as entertainment or business? (K Jones, 1984).

Fourth, the simulation is not implemented for students to meet a success criterion. That is, students should not be evaluated as to whether or not they followed a particular course of action or whether a particular objective is or is not met. Instead, the emphasis is on the use of language as a functional tool.

The use of technology

As in other subject areas, computer-managed videodisc technology is proposed as a new dimension in the development of simulations for language learning. One project being undertaken at Massachusetts Institute of Technology is developing experimental software prototypes in five languages (Higgins and Morgenstern, 1990). One of the prototypes is *No Recuerdo* (I Can't Remember) which is designed for intermediate-level Spanish learners.

In *No Recuerdo*, the learner communicates with two protagonists to help them recall lost memories (Oxford and Crookall, 1990). One route through the program is that of helping a South American scientist (an amnesia victim) reconstruct events that involve a kidnapping, an illicit entanglement and an experiment in genetic engineering with potentially catastrophic outcomes (Higgins and Morgenstern, 1990, p 187). However, before access to these important memories is accomplished, the learner must keep the scientist talking about non-threatening topics such as the weather and food. Words that occur during these 'conversations', however, open gateways to the other forgotten areas.

The information on the videodisc includes both visual and auditory material. Included are still photos, short video and film segments and text overlay on some of the materials. However, the learner *must type his or her input into the 'conversation'*.

The material blends fictional and factual elements and is a move-based program like the adventure games developed for popular entertainment. It is also an example of interactive fiction in that the learner controls the plot development and interacts with the protagonists. However, the merging of fact and fiction in interactive lessons should be seriously examined from a pedagogical perspective. First, how does the learner know when fact stops and fiction begins? Second, consider, for example, the increase in power of the lesson if historically accurate scenes and situations were the bases for the lesson. History contains ample drama that is often stranger than fiction. Furthermore, students placed in historical situations to interact with historical characters might pose a variety of strategies for resolving a difficult situation. Their strategies could then be examined as to probability of success, given the climate of the times.

Although videodisc technology has the capability to provide reactions to learner input that the learner can see and hear, the primary requirement for reality of function – human interaction – is lacking. Therefore, language exercises that make use of videodisc technology are more appropriately described as problem-solving exercises with simulated materials.

MAJOR DESIGN ISSUES

Important design issues are the specific uses of language required in the simulation, the ways that language use may be analysed, the nature of the basic situation and types of follow-up activities.

Specific uses of language

As indicated in the prior section, simulations for communication may be used for either of two general purposes. One is to stretch the participants' communicative skills. In fulfilling this purpose, simulations may be chosen in which oral language serves one or more primary uses. For example, one use of language is to convey and/or to obtain key information essential to solving a problem. Another is to use language to establish a positive emotional reaction, such as a feeling of confidence.

Five specific uses of oral language and simulations are summarized in Table 9.1. One purpose of this listing is to identify the primary language use or uses prior to planning instruction. The rationale for such an approach is to ensure that the exercise targets the particular skills of interest and to assist in matching simulations to the language skills and needs of the participants.

The language uses illustrated in Table 9.1 are not necessarily mutually exclusive. When medical interns interview simulated patients, for example, the purposes are to obtain accurate information from the patient, to convey a sense of empathy and to instil a sense of confidence in the patient in the intern's skills.

Conveying or abstracting information

A simulation that illustrates the importance of accurately conveying and/or obtaining information establishes a situation in which those skills are essential for success. Also, like many situations in everyday life, individuals may have only fragments of information which, when

Table 9.1 *Specific Uses of Oral Language Represented in Simulations*

USE	SIMULATION
1. Conveying or abstracting information	*Space Crash*
2. Using new vocabulary to plan or to develop activities	*The Arts Centre*
3. Developing communications/ information for dissemination	*Radio Covingham* *People in the News*
4. Using language to establish or to change opinions	*St Philip* *The Bridge*
5. Using language to establish positive emotional reactions	*Patient interviews conducted by the 'family doctor'; simulations of political caucuses or rallies*

pieced together with other sources, provide coherent information for a course of action. The key, of course, is making sure that all vital information is brought to the fore and considered.

One example is the imaginative simulation *Space Crash*. The five participants (Andro, Betelg, Cassi, Draco and Enid) are members of a space crew stranded on the strange planet Dy. Their task is to stay alive and each role card contains items essential to the crew's survival. They must communicate this information to each other and plan their journey across the planet to find food and water.

However, the task is not as straightforward as it seems. The information on each role card is two or three bits of unrelated information which must be integrated with items from other role cards in order to understand the message.

For example, Andro's card states that the crew has no food or water and nothing to carry water in. However, the Dyans, the natives of the planet, can show them the way to the radio station where food and water can be found. Cassi's card states that the crew can live three days without water; on Dy the valleys are not usually near the hills; the only other water on Dy is at the radio station; and the mast can be seen from the top of the hill. Betelg's card contains the information that the crew cannot move diagonally and the notes on the edges of the map squares indicate what can be seen one day's walk away (except for the hill which is two days' walk away) (K Jones, 1982, p 54). This organization of key information establishes a situation in which success depends on careful listening as well as clear communication.

Using new vocabulary to plan or develop activities
An example of applying new vocabulary to a problem that requires discussion and group decision-making is *The Arts Centre* (L Jones, 1983). The centre consists of a theatre, a cinema, a concert hall, a restaurant, a bar and a large area inside the main entrance appropriate for exhibitions and other activities (p 39). Participants take roles as members of four different groups of staff at the centre – theatre, concert hall, restaurant and cinema and exhibitions. Each group is headed by a manager who sits on the board of directors.

The task for each staff group is to plan the activities of the centre for the next six months, paying particular attention to the group's own special area (L Jones, 1983). Although the centre is subsidized by the local county, the subsidy covers only 40 per cent of the costs. The remainder must be earned from profits.

A floor plan of the centre, an organizational chart of the staff and a flyer announcing one month's activities at the centre are the materials given to the participants. Announcements on the flyer serve to stimulate the ideas of participants. An 'Under 16s Disco' is scheduled in the concert hall for one Thursday night; this month is designated as Italian month in the restaurant; the restaurant offers a business lunch five days a week; Saturdays in the concert hall are billed as 'Kids' Stuff'; and so on.

The vocabulary needed for the simulation consists of the terms associated with the different kinds of entertainment, publicity and finance. Thus, the vocabulary ranges from dubbed film, chamber music, light comedy and pantomime to à la carte, set meal, sponsor, creditor, in the red and in the black.

Developing information for dissemination

Typical situations that make use of writing and editing skills in addition to deciding priorities are those in which newspaper items or radio broadcasts are developed. In *Radio Covingham*, the task is to develop a broadcast of 10 minutes by a certain time. The broadcast, 'News and Views at 7', features views about current news items, therefore interviews and comments must be prepared. Also, news items keep coming in up to the time of the broadcast. Thus, editing and rewriting are also required of the participants.

Another broadcast simulation uses three teams, each working on a news magazine programme, *People in the News* (L Jones, 1983). Each team works for one of three radio stations that serve different audiences. Members of EBC-1's audience are factory workers who are interested in people-oriented stories, not long news reports. They read *The Sun* or the *Daily Mirror*. In contrast, EBC-2's audience consists of white-collar workers with a good education. They want information and entertainment in equal portions and they read the *Daily Mail* or the *Daily Express*. In contrast, managers and teachers are the audience for EBC-3 who want the facts about current issues presented in an interesting way. They read *The Guardian* or *The Times* (L Jones, 1983, p 36). Like *Radio Covingham*, news items and telephoned reports arrive until broadcast time.

Using language to establish or to change opinions

A simulation that relies on language for establishing or changing opinions must pose an issue on which participants take different sides. The skills required in the resolution of the issue are negotiating, debating and persuasion. *St Philip*, discussed in Chapter 8, is an example in which these skills are important. However, one limitation of *St Philip* is that the hotel developers cannot participate in the parliamentary discussion. In a simulation selected for communication, all roles should be participatory throughout the exercise.

Another example is the simulation *The Bridge* (L Jones, 1983). The local government is planning to replace the old chain ferry across the entrance to Merryton Harbour with a suspension toll bridge. Participants take the roles of different community members who are in favour of the bridge, oppose the project or are undecided (p 15). Information for the participants includes a summary of the costs and income for the ferry for three years, the costs of the construction, a map of the area and three newspaper articles.

One of the articles discusses the rare Deptford warbler which, although almost extinct, has just begun to breed again. The warbler has selected the Netherfield Heath Nature Reserve which is near the point where the bridge is to be built. The shy birds have been driven away from other nesting sites by the noise and pollution of motor traffic.

After a period of time during which the opposers and supporters of the bridge attempt to persuade the undecided townspeople, a public meeting is held. The simulation ends with the vote on the proposed bridge.

Using language to establish positive emotional reactions
Establishing positive emotional reactions may be a secondary purpose of a simulation. Teams preparing the radio broadcasts for *People in the News*, for instance, are seeking positive reactions to the programme from their intended audience. As already indicated, patient interviews conducted by interns in the role of the family doctor are evaluated for the sense of confidence and security that is instilled in the 'patients'.

On occasion, establishing a positive emotional reaction may be the major goal of language use, with information dissemination or some other purpose a secondary goal. Examples include political caucuses or rallies where a group is attempting to 'sell' a particular political candidate to the others or a sales team developing publicity or advertising for a particular product or event.

Analysing language use

One of the general purposes of implementing language skills/communication simulations is that of analysing language use by the participants. This use of simulations provides information to the teacher for structuring subsequent instruction. The simulation is tape-recorded and the teacher may conduct the analysis by playing the recording or by reading a typed script prepared from the recording.

Two types of language analysis have been suggested by K Jones (1982). One is functional analysis, which is somewhat subjective. Functional analysis includes information such as the use of different techniques (signposting, questioning and categorical statements), contextual appropriateness and others (p 57). Another approach is for the teacher, prior to implementing the situation, to make a list of the types of expressions that are functional in the particular exercise. For example, five types of useful expressions in *The Bridge* are presenting a point of view, disagreeing, presenting counter-arguments, raising objections and expressing indecision (L Jones, 1983, p 16). In a simulation in which the focus is on group planning, categories of useful language include stating an opinion, finding out other people's views, expressing complete or partial agreement, expressing disagreement and requesting clarification (L Jones, 1983, p 24).

For radio broadcasts, an important type of language is the transitions between programme items to create a sense of smoothness. Examples are '. . . and now back to John at the newsdesk' (L Jones, 1983, p 10) and 'Now from wild and windy weather to wild animals. The giraffes at Wessex Zoo have . . .' or 'Now from high winds to long necks: the giraffes at Wessex Zoo have . . .' (p 34).

The purpose of a prepared list of types of language important in the particular simulation is to provide guidelines for analysing students' language during the exercise. Such a list contributes to a comprehensive review of language use and assists in preventing omissions in the analysis.

The other type of language analysis is grammatical. Errors in both grammar and pronunciation are noted and are addressed in subsequent lessons. Grammatical analyses may be made from typed scripts of the simulation and are useful when a class goal is to develop correct language use. However, if the primary goal is that of improving fluency in public for students who can speak correctly, grammatical analysis may not be needed.

Nature of the situation

In order to provide a language-intensive experience for the participants, simulations for communication should fulfil several criteria. First, the rules should be simple and easy to follow. Second, the background material should be minimal and easy to read. The notes for participants in *Space Crash*, for instance, inform them of their situation and that their goal is survival. The purpose is to allow participants to focus on their tasks or goals in the simulation without first becoming side-tracked on deciphering or interpreting written documents.

Third, the situation should pose a challenge but not a threat to the participants. The simulations that are particularly effective are those that include a mechanism that signals a conclusion to the exercise. The time limits in *Radio Covingham* and *The Crisis Game* are examples. In contrast, *Space Crash* ends when the crew 'dies' (the typical conclusion) or reaches food and water and *The Bridge* ends with the vote at the public meeting.

Planning post-simulation activities

The types of follow-up activities selected for language skills simulations depend, in part, on the purpose for which the exercise is implemented. The simulated patient interviews conducted by interns, for example, are an important component in developing essential skills for future doctors. These interviews are videotaped and the instructor reviews the tape with the intern, citing strengths and weaknesses.

Feedback is also obtained from the 'patient' on his or her reactions.

In other settings in which communication skills are the focus, the group discussion is the key to learning. K Jones (1982, p 9) notes that participants vividly remember the ideas and thoughts they tried to communicate, the ways they attempted to convey their ideas, the reactions and the results. The vividness of these memories is the impetus for learning.

The discussion can explore ways to agree, disagree, bring up a point for consideration and so on, based on the teacher's notes of the difficulties identified from the tape-recording or typed script. Also, as students become more sophisticated, the discussion can explore points at which listeners might have asked for clarification or for further information to prevent receiving inadequate or inaccurate information. However, it is important that the discussion should not be a repeat of the events or arguments used in the simulation (K Jones, 1982, p 117).

In addition to discussions about the simulation, L Jones (1983) suggests that simulations for upper-intermediate and advanced students may include written assignments. Two follow-up assignments to *The Bridge* are 1) to write a letter to the Editor of the *Meryton Evening News* expressing an opinion about the outcome of the public meeting; and 2) to write a summary of the advantages and disadvantages of building the North Point bridge (p 22).

Simulations for language learning are not isolated experiences. They may be incorporated with other language activities, such as keeping a weekly journal of thoughts and impressions of class events and other simulations that gradually expand the students' repertoire of skills.

In summary, simulations can provide a variety of language experiences for students. Of importance, however, is that a comfortable climate is established in the classroom and penalties are not attached to errors. In this way, the student can experience a rich variety of goal-directed situations on any of several levels of competence.

EVALUATING SIMULATIONS FOR LANGUAGE SKILLS/COMMUNICATION

Step 1: Identify the specific purpose or purposes that may be met by the simulation.
- What are the functional uses of communication that the simulation may fulfil (see Table 9.1)?
- Does the situation tap a variety of skills or only a few?

Step 2: Determine the nature of the situation.
- Does the simulation involve every role prescribed in the exercise?
- Is the proposed task likely to be a challenge but not a threat for the participants?

- Do students have opportunities to be creative in the simulation?
- Can students at different levels of competence participate in the exercise or are high-ability students likely to dominate the action?

REFERENCES

Hannay, D R (1980) 'Teaching interviewing with simulated patients', *Medical Education*, **14**, 246-8.

Higgins, L J and Morgenstern, D (1990) 'Simulations on computers: Elements and examples', in Crookall, D and Oxford, R L (eds) *Simulation, Gaming and Language Learning*, 183-9, New York: Newbury House.

Jones, K (1982) *Simulations in Language Teaching*, Cambridge: Cambridge University Press.

Jones, K (1984) 'Simulations versus professional educators' in Jaques, D and Tippev, E (eds), Learning for the Future with Games and Simulations, 45-50, Loughborough University: SAGSET.

Jones, L (1983) *Eight Simulations*, Cambridge: Cambridge University Press.

McAvoy, B R (1988) 'Teaching clinical skills to medical students: The use of simulated patients and videotaping in general practice', *Medical Education*, **22**, 193-9.

Oxford, R and Crookall, D (1990) 'Learning strategies, Making language learning more effective through simulation/gaming', in Crookall, D and Oxford, R (eds) *Simulation, Gaming and Language Learning*, 109-17, New York: Newbury House.

Sanson-Fisher, R W and Poole, A D (1980) 'Simulated patients and the assessment of medical students' interpersonal skills', *Medical Education*, 14, 249-53.

Scarcella, R and Crookall, D (1990) 'Simulation/gaming and language acquisition', in Crookall, D and Oxford, R (eds) *Simulation, Gaming and Language Learning*, 223-30, New York: Newbury House.

Scarcella, R and Stern, S L (1990) 'Reading, writing, and literature: Integrating language skills' in Crookall, D and Oxford, R (eds) *Simulation, Gaming and Language Learning*, 119-24, New York: Newbury House.

10 Empathy/insight simulations

Empathy and insight, like complex language and communication skills, are uniquely human traits. The circumstances of modern life, however, including the fast pace and competing demands, are not conducive to the development of sensitivity and empathy.

Webster's Dictionary defines empathy as 'the capacity for participation in another's feelings'. The difficulties involved in acquiring empathy are illustrated in the 1991 Hollywood film, *The Doctor*, starring William Hurt. The film is based on the real-life story of a doctor who changed his attitudes toward patients after suffering a life-threatening illness and experiencing the reactions of the health-care system as a patient.

Simulations considered to be empathy/insight simulations place participants in situations in which they experience the same emotions as those experienced by a particular individual or reference group. An example is *Me The Slow Learner* in which teachers and prospective teachers experience the same continuous failures and frustrations as learning–disabled students.

OVERVIEW

In the early years of development, empathy and insight were viewed as typical expectations for many simulations. Thus, the issue of simulation characteristics that specifically contribute to the development of empathy is a relatively new one in simulation design.

Early developments

In July 1977, seven broad communication purposes for 'gaming/ simulations' were identified at a conference on Global Interactions and Gaming/Simulations held in Nijmagen, the Netherlands. The first purpose was: '(A) *Motivation/sensitivity* – to help participants develop empathy by experiencing the roles of those with value orientations and constraints different from their own' (Hasell, 1980, p 287).

The implicit assumption in many early exercises was that empathy could be fostered by placing a participant in a different role in an appropriate context. Some exercises also incorporated gaming elements into the structure. For example, *Ghetto* is described as a simulation 'designed to sensitize its players to the emotional, physical and social world the disadvantaged inhabit' (Edwards, 1980, p 343). Individuals assumed the names and ages of different ghetto residents and attempted to improve their lives by investing hours (poker chips) in various activities and collecting as many reward points as possible. Chance events that negated 'investments' and reduced reward points were expected to produce frustration in the players similar to the frustrations experienced by the disadvantaged. However, the exercise (both the board and computerized versions) is a game. In the computerized form, *Ghetto* is a variable-assignment exercise like *Oregon Trail* in which the outcomes are dominated by random events.

A different approach to the development of empathy/insight was taken by Shirts (1969) in *Starpower*. Participants in the simulation believe that they are playing a game that involves trading chips of different values. They are told that the three individuals with the highest scores at the end of trading will be the winners.

After one round of trading, participants with the highest scores are placed in a group called the Squares. The middle third of the scorers form a group called the Circles and the lowest third are the Triangles. A second round of trading then takes place. However, events in the exercise depend on the Squares emerging from the second round as the high scorers. Unknown to the players, the game is structured so that the Squares are the high scorers for the second round.

At this point, the director gives the Squares the privilege of making all the rules for the game because ostensibly they have worked so hard. The Circles and Triangles may suggest rules by submitting them in writing to the Squares. Also, the Squares may be quietly told that they can make rules such as all chips should be distributed equally, Circles and Triangles must trade with a Square even if they don't want to and so on.

The likely outcome is that the Squares make stringent rules that protect their status. Circles and Triangles express their frustration in any of several ways – protesting, organizing against the Squares, refusing to play and so on. The director stops the exercise when the Squares have formulated rules so one-sided that the Circles and Triangles turn against the Squares. In other words, the exercise is stopped when the Squares have abused their power and the Circles and Triangles either give up or defy the Squares.

Until the final minutes, participants believe that they are playing a game. However, the 'game' activities are set up in order to establish a three-tiered situation in which the 'rich get richer'. The circumstances are orchestrated to provide a situation in which the Squares are given licence to make rules that benefit their group.

Starpower is an ingenious exercise in that conflict between the groups is established. However, the exercise contains a design flaw that generates undesirable effects when implemented. This problem is discussed in the section on design issues.

Major characteristics

The key characteristic of empathy/insight simulations is that participants are placed in an unpleasant, confusing or humiliating situation and they are powerless to change the circumstances. In *Me The Slow Learner*, for example, participants are unable to perform successfully on a series of classroom tasks that are nearly impossible because of several situational circumstances. Although participants exert great effort, they are unable to be successful.

Empathy/insight simulations are similar to single-agenda simulations in that participants are placed in situations that essentially trap them. However, the key difference lies in the nature of the constraints that trap the participants. In the single-agenda simulation, participants are trapped by their own assumptions and behaviours. In other words, given enough time, participants can escape from or mitigate the situation by changing their behaviour. In *The Numbers Game*, for example, participants eventually settle down and accomplish the task. In *Talking Rocks*, the Eagle people, after some trial and error, begin to develop picture messages for the other groups.

In contrast, in the empathy/insight simulation, participants are trapped by constraints over which they have no control. Thus, there is no escape. The near-impossible tasks set for the 'learning–disabled students' in *Me The Slow Learner*, for example, are not accomplished by exerting greater effort or by changing strategies.

The effect of this design feature is that, typically, empathy/insight simulations are more intense experiences than other simulations. The inability of the participants to influence their circumstances contributes to their increased frustration and, in some cases, rebellion.

In other words, simulations developed to foster empathy are inherently the most emotion-laden of the social-process simulations. The greater the intensity of the frustration or shock, the greater the opportunity for reflection and rethinking. However, extreme frustration is likely to be accompanied by other negative emotions – anger, loss of self-esteem and resentment. The potential for setting in motion strong negative feelings that may not be dissipated easily or may be channelled later into inappropriate behaviours implies that both the design and implementation of empathy/insight simulations should be undertaken with care. More importantly, such simulations should not be used with children.

Another key characteristic of empathy simulations is that they are only the first step in the development of empathy and insight. The emotions generated in the simulations must be explored and then channelled in positive directions. In other words, participant reactions in the simulation serve only as the impetus for growth and development.

MAJOR DESIGN ISSUES

Several issues are important in the development of empathy simulations. Included are a) basic requirements; b) the nature of the basic situation; c) the nature of participant reactions; d) post-simulation activities; and e) the cost/benefit ratio.

Basic requirements

Empathy/insight simulations place participants in frustrating or confusing situations that their efforts are powerless to change. The intention is for the participants to experience the particular frustrations and/or negative emotions felt by a particular individual or group in society as a first step in developing new ways of thinking about certain events and situations.

One example is the exercise devised by a high school teacher of a marriage and family course for high school students. She believed it was important for teenagers to experience the continuing and ever-present responsibility of parenthood. The key was to identify an ongoing situation in which the students could experience the restriction on freedom and the attentiveness that parenthood requires.

An exercise was devised in which the 'parents' must care for a 'baby' over a two- to three-week period. They were never to leave the 'baby' unless a responsible sitter could be found; otherwise, one or the other of the couple was required to stay with the baby or take it with them. The 'baby' was a 10-pound sack of flour. The parents could also not be careless with baby, dropping it or otherwise damaging it in transport, because they then lost the child and could not succeed in the exercise. The 'parents' in this exercise experience reality of function in that they encounter the essence of parenthood – that of an ever-present responsibility that cannot be ignored.

The design of empathy/insight simulations should be consistent with two basic requirements. First, participants should not be misled about the nature of the situation nor tricked in any way into executing behaviours that are later criticized. Second, like other simulations, empathy/insight simulations are not games and care should be taken that participants do not view them as games.

Starpower, however, violates both requirements. First, participants are told they are participating in a game and that the three highest scores will win. When given an opportunity to make the rules, the *Squares* do so in a way that ensures that three of their group will be the winners. There is no difference between this behaviour and the behaviour of bankrupting one's friends in *Monopoly*. Both actions are entirely legitimate *in a game situation*. (Recall from Chapter 1 that a game is a fantasy world unto itself. It must be internally consistent, but it is not a representation or reflection of the real world.)

At the point that the Circles and Triangles rebel or otherwise refuse to cooperate with the stringent rules adopted by the Squares, the game is halted by the director. The post-simulation discussion then focuses on the behaviour of the Squares and the reactions of the Circles and Triangles. However, *the behaviour of the Squares is extrapolated into the real world as though the Squares were not playing a game*. They have, in other words, been tricked. In fact, the *Director's Instructions* includes the statement that the Squares sometimes have difficulty in admitting that they abused their power (Shirts, 1969 p 18). They are quite correct – their behaviour was appropriate for the game they believed they were playing.

Director's Instructions also describes the concepts that typically emerge from the post-simulation discussion. Two of the concepts are '1. Each of us may be more vulnerable to the temptation to abuse power than we realize' (p 18) and '2. To change behavior, it may be necessary to change the system in which that behavior occurs' (p 19). Other concepts are that individuals who feel powerless are not likely to participate in an endeavour; rules that lack legitimacy are not obeyed; the concept of 'fairness' is viewed differently by those in power and others; and those who are promoted tend not to remember people they left behind (pp 20–21).

In other words, participants have been asked to judge the Squares' game behaviour as though it were real-world behaviour. Participants are not sophisticated enough to understand the differences between games and simulations and thus do not question the transfer.

A more serious problem, however, is that issues of trust may be raised: Susan (a Triangle) may wonder if Diane (a Square) is entirely trustworthy. Hard feelings generated by the exercise may persist into the educational or work setting.

Therefore, selection of an empathy/insight simulation should be based, in part, on congruence with the two basic requirements. They ensure the integrity of behaviour when participants conscientiously carry out their functions.

Nature of the basic situation

The tasks and context developed for empathy simulations must meet three important criteria identified by Thatcher (1983). First and foremost, the situation must prevent the participant from escaping. The term 'escape', however, does not refer to physical exit. Instead, it refers to the mental and/or emotional withdrawal that occurs when one comes out of a role without actually leaving the activity.

In other words, the participants must 'not be able to "come out" of the session in any way unless they actually opt out by leaving the room or, alternatively, refuse overtly or covertly to participate in the activity' (Thatcher, 1983, p 14). Therefore, in order to prevent mental or emotional withdrawal, participants are not assigned roles as the individuals with whom they are to establish empathy. If roles are assigned in which participants role-play mental or physical handicaps, they can 'come out' of the activity fairly easily.

Another reason for not assigning roles as disadvantaged students is that participants lack the essential understandings and knowledge to function in the role. Although participants may conscientiously attempt to behave as learning-disabled children or inner-city homeless teenagers, the activity is a play-acting experience for the participants. Such a situation does not facilitate learning and also may lead to superficial views and actions. In other words, although participants may expend great effort attempting to think and react like underprivileged children or minority inner-city teenagers the experience lacks reality of function for them.

Therefore, empathy/insight simulations place participants, as a group, into a context that imposes a particular set of aversive contingencies. The circumstances are such that participants are unable to change them. Thus, they can only respond to the situation in which they find themselves and their coping mechanisms are taxed by the experience. In other words, the contingencies of reinforcement are altered so that participant behaviours are ineffective.

Participants in *Me The Slow Learner* are learning-disabled children who are faced with problems to solve. However, they are first fitted with devices that produce some disability such as glasses that produce tunnel vision or colour blindness and impediments to hearing and physical movement. In addition, insufficient time and the unclear presentation of the tasks combine with the participant's disability to make the problems impossible. Since individuals are not permitted to talk to each other during the classroom 'activities', they have no choice but to keep trying the tasks or to sit silently waiting for the ordeal to end.

The second important characteristic is that the developing situation should be cumulative (Thatcher, 1983). For example, the 'parents', in caring for the flour sack 'baby' experience continued frustration as the early days of their 'parenthood' stretches into weeks.

The cumulative experience for participants in *Me The Slow Learner* is that of continuing failure on six problem-solving tasks. Moreover, the sense of frustration is intensified by the participants' knowledge that the activities could be completed given greater clarity in the task, or if the participant did not have a disability (Thatcher, 1983, p 15).

Third, the simulation must present 'in a condensed and intensified form, many of the major elements of the complex system which in actuality is extended over months and often years' (Thatcher, 1983, p 15). *Me The Slow Learner* addresses this requirement in three ways. In addition to experiencing specific disadvantages, participants are subjected to derogatory comments by their 'teachers' (project staff) and public scoring of their efforts which reinforce the sense of failure. These events represent the reactions of the world at large to disabled people that occur in the form of derogatory comments, innuendos or facial reactions (Thatcher, 1983, p 15).

Furthermore, some of the tasks have been re-designed to appear as they would to learning–disabled children. Letters and words are reversed and parts of words are omitted in the technical passage that the participants are to read. Similarly, the mathematics task uses unfamiliar terms which add to the complexity of the problem (Thatcher, 1983).

In addition to the design characteristics identified by Thatcher (1983), exercises should not be designed that set groups against each other. One shortcoming of *Starpower* is this very feature. As already stated, one problem is that the feelings of the Circles and Triangles may carry over to future interactions. That is, Circles and Triangles may feel betrayed by a friend who was a Square. If strong negative effects are to be experienced, the simulation should be designed so that all participants experience them.

Nature of participant reactions

Participant reactions occur at two stages in the administration of an empathy simulation. The first is during the exercise itself and the second may occur from one day to several weeks after the experience.

Reactions by participants to the aversive circumstances in empathy simulations vary on at least three dimensions. They are a) the degree of frustration; b) the complexity of the emotional reaction; and c) the target of participant emotions.

The extent of the frustration may range from low to high and the level may vary with different participants in the same simulation. Some of the teenage girls caring for the flour sack 'babies' accommodated fairly well to the new responsibility, while others experienced high levels of frustration.

In contrast, *Me The Slow Learner* is designed specifically to produce high frustration levels in all participants. Further, the extent of the difficulties faced by the participants interacts with their background to produce a complex matrix of emotions – anger, hostility, lack of motivation and, in some participants, withdrawal.

The teachers and prospective teachers who take part in the simulation are academically-able individuals who may not have experienced serious difficulties in learning. They are accustomed to achieving and the awareness that a clear task presentation or removal of their disability would make achievement possible contributes to their negative emotions. They also are somewhat shocked that they cannot overcome the circumstances to accomplish the otherwise simple tasks. In other words, their accepted beliefs about themselves as competent and able to overcome obstacles through hard work is contradicted by their incompetence in the simulation. The sense of shock generated by this situation is essential, according to Thatcher (1983), because it is the basis of rethinking that leads to empathy.

Simulation designers and administrators should also be alert to the direction of the participants' emotional reactions. That is, participants may become angry at themselves and/or suffer temporary loss of self-esteem or they may vent their frustrations on other participants or the simulation directors. The teenage 'parents', for example, sometimes argued about whose turn it was to care for the 'baby', and some blamed each other for not succeeding in the exercise.

In contrast, the simulation directors for *Me The Slow Learner* are the source of some of the participants' difficulties. They nag the 'learning--disabled students' and publicly attach low marks to their work. During at least two administrations, the directors experienced the feeling of losing control of the class. This feeling was related to the loss of discipline and the continued deterioration of the participants' behaviour (Thatcher, 1983). It is important to recognize that these reactions are not unusual and administrators should be prepared to address them in post-simulation activities.

Post-simulation activities

The simulation experience is only one phase in student learning. Subsequent activities are required to build on the processes set in motion during the simulation. (Chapter 11 presents the experiential learning models that address the different experiences essential to resolving social conflict and reorganizing one's intuitive ways of thinking).

Empathy/insight simulations are intense experiences. Typically, participants are placed in a situation in which their accepted beliefs about themselves are contradicted. In *Me The Slow Learner*, participants' views of themselves as competent individuals who can overcome obstacles through hard work and extra effort are not true in the simulation. They experience the phenomenon referred to by Piaget (1972) as cognitive conflict or disequilibrium. That is, they are faced with two contradictory views of themselves – competence that overcomes obstacles and incompetence in the face of difficulties.

Therefore, participants should not be expected to articulate the depth of their feelings immediately after the experience. In-service teachers who were participants in *Me The Slow Learner*, for example, seemed to require several weeks to process the full impact of the simulation (Thatcher, 1983). Therefore, several activities should be planned to provide opportunities for the participants to explore their reactions, the nature of the context and/or system that precipitated those reactions and the implications.

In simulations that generate a range of intense emotions, a short informal break without the game administrators should be scheduled between the end of the simulation and the first post-simulation discussion (Thatcher and Robinson, 1990). This brief coffee break allows the participants to release their pent-up frustration, some of which may be felt toward the administrators.

Four specific activities are suggested by Thatcher and Robinson (1990, p 266) for a post-simulation discussion. First, participants complete a questionnaire that focuses each participant's memory of the experience. Second, the game administrator invites participants to make immediate comments. This activity permits strong reactions or points to be released by the participants.

Third, the discussion proceeds to a more orderly examination of the participants' reactions. The significance of different kinds of behaviour during the simulation, such as giggling and aggression, are also explored. Finally, the discussion broadens to include the implications of the experience.

Partly as the result of the intensity of the reactions in the simulation, participants are likely to continue to reflect and to develop new ideas in the weeks after the simulation. Therefore, an instructor–student conference should be scheduled a week or two after the simulation as well as a second group discussion a few weeks later.

The intention of the empathy/insight simulation is to influence participants' decision-making in some way. Therefore, activities should also be implemented in which similar and/or related situations, and possible actions and/or decisions of the participants for countering similar negative situations, may be examined.

Other planned discussions following *Me The Slow Learner*, for example, may include topics such as the different ways that low achievers are sometimes treated in the classroom and the differences between proactive and reactive teachers. Specifically, low achievers are sometimes seated farther from the teacher and/or in groups, less work is expected of them and less attention is paid to them. Included are less eye contact, fewer opportunities to respond to teacher questions, less time to answer questions and so on (Good, 1980, p 88). These teachers are referred to by Good as 'reactive' because they over-react to students perceived as low achievers. In contrast, proactive teachers build classroom structures in which the needs of low achievers can be met without ignoring the needs of other students.

Subsequent class discussions can then address ways that the teachers can structure their classrooms to provide for multiple learning needs. In this way, the growth experiences set in motion by the simulation begin to be developed.

Cost/benefit ratio

Empathy/insight simulations are risk-taking exercises in that they place participants in situations that generate negative reactions. Therefore, both the design and implementation should be undertaken from the perspective of a clear rationale for subjecting participants to an aversive experience.

In other words, the primary question is, 'Is the pay-off worth the negative effect experienced by the participants?' If the negative effect is relatively mild *and* the exercise makes a point that is important in their lives, the answer is likely to be in the affirmative. An example is the teenage 'parents' caring for their flour-sack 'babies'. Teenage pregnancy is a growing problem in the United States. To the extent that simulations can counter the naive belief that having a baby is like having a doll that breathes, they may be a step in addressing the problem.

Simulations that produce intense and complex emotional reactions, such as loss of self-esteem and/or anger that may be directed to any of a number of individuals, should not be used in the classroom or work setting unless two criteria are met. First, is the anticipated empathy that is to be developed related to key decisions in participants' lives that should be addressed or understood in new ways? In other words, does the exercise represent a possible pivotal point in the decision-making activities of the participants?

For example, *Starpower* was developed to demonstrate the abuses of power. Setting aside for the moment the design flaws within the exercise, what post-simulation decisions are to be undertaken in a different way as a result of participation in the exercise? Are the participants to become more vigilant citizens in monitoring their government officials for the abuse of power? Or are they to understand the psychological dynamics of power so as to recognize its early stages? Or are they to experience the effects of discrimination so that they can call this problem to the attention of government agencies and others? In other words, the post-simulation decision-making that the new insight is expected to influence is not clear.

The second criterion that should be met is to determine if the simulation is the most effective mechanism by which the intended change in thinking may be met. Considering each of the possible purposes for *Starpower* in turn, can other experiences influence the subsequent behaviour of the participants?

Becoming a more vigilant citizen, for example, may be accomplished by discussing ways that government fails to be regulated, analysing contemporary examples of corruption that have been discovered and writing letters to elected representatives and other follow-up activities. Similarly, examining in detail the careers of public servants who became mesmerized by power is appropriate for the second purpose. Finally, experiencing the effects of discrimination calls for a different kind of interactive exercise.

Me The Slow Learner, in contrast, was developed for a specific purpose and was based on the experiences of a particular group of teachers. That is, the teachers who were most successful with less-able pupils had experienced difficulty at some point in their own schooling (Thatcher and Robinson, 1990, p 264). In overcoming the difficulty they had acquired practical insight into the problems and feelings associated with learning difficulties.

The specifications for the simulation, therefore, were that teachers who do not have obvious learning problems should experience the difficulties of learning–disabled pupils as a first step in learning to work with and manage these children (Thatcher & Robinson, 1990, p 265).

Thus, the criterion that an empathy simulation should be related to key decisions in the participants' lives is met. The second criterion is also met. The objective is to generate the feelings, reactions and anxieties that are experienced by less-able children in the school environment. Thus, a 'walk in my shoes' exercise is needed. However, the benefits of the simulation are realized only in the growth experiences developed in the post-simulation activities.

In summary, empathy/insight simulations are powerful exercises that, properly designed and implemented, can fulfil a unique purpose in the educational setting.

EVALUATING EMPATHY/INSIGHT SIMULATIONS

Step 1: Analyse the nature of the basic situation.
- Are participants placed in a situation from which they cannot escape?
- Is the situation credible for the intended participants?
- Does the situation avoid tricking the participants in any way?
- Does the exercise avoid assigning roles for which participants lack relevant experience?

Step 2: Determine the intensity of the experience.
- What are the specific components of the simulation that generate negative reactions?
- Is the simulation likely to generate mild frustration or intensely negative emotions?
- Is the experience likely to generate temporary loss of self-esteem?

- Does the simulation present the elements of a complex system in a condensed and intensified form?
- Are the effects of the experience likely to be cumulative?

Step 3: Review the post-simulation activities (see Chapter 11 for a more detailed discussion).

- Do the activities include two group processing sessions a few weeks apart?
- Is at least one instructor-student conference scheduled?
- What homework assignments and class activities are developed to build on the simulation experience?
- Do the scheduled activities contribute to a sense of empathy?

Step 4: Determine the cost/benefit ratio.

- Is the empathy that is expected related to decisions in participants' lives?
- Can the expected empathy be fostered in other ways?

REFERENCES

Edwards, J (1980) 'Review of *Ghetto*', in Horn, R E and Cleaves, A (eds) *The Guide to Simulations/Games for Education and Training*, (4th edn), 343-4, Beverly Hills, CA: Sage Publications.

Good, T (1980) 'Classroom expectations: Teacher-pupil interactions', in McMillan, J H (ed) *The Social Psychology of School Learning*, 79-122, New York: Academic Press.

Hasell, M J (1980) 'Urban gaming simulations: An evaluation', in Horn, R E and Cleaves, A (eds) *The Guide to Simulations/Games for Education and Training*, (4th edn), 286-303, Beverly Hills, CA: Sage Publications.

Piaget, J (1972) *The Principles of Genetic Epistemology*, New York: Basic.

Shirts, R G (1969) *Director's Instructions: STAR POWER* La Jolla, CA: Simile II.

Thatcher, D (1983) 'A consideration of the use of simulation for the promotion of empathy in the training for the caring professions - "Me The Slow Learner", a case study', *Simulation/Games for Learning*, **13**, 1, 10-16.

Thatcher, D and Robinson, J (1990) 'Me The Slow Learner: reflections eight years on from its original design'. *Simulation/Games for Learning*, **20**, 3, 264-75.

11 The role of post-simulation activities

A simulation is an experiential exercise in that participants step into assigned roles, accept the responsibilities and constraints and work through the problems and difficulties that arise in the execution of the roles.

A well-designed simulation captures the attention, thoughts and efforts of the participants and often involves their feelings as well. As a result, participants have no opportunity during the simulation to reflect on either their own actions, assumptions or beliefs or those of others in the exercise. To be maximally effective, the participant's experience should lead to both reflection on the experience and to new patterns of thinking. However, such learning cannot be left to chance or to a brief post-exercise discussion. Instead, post-simulation activities should be planned as carefully and thoughtfully as the simulation itself.

MODELS OF EXPERIENTIAL LEARNING

Two models of learning are relevant to a discussion of learning through simulations. They are the group-dynamics model developed by Kurt Lewin, a Gestalt theorist, and the cognitive-development model developed by Jean Piaget, a Swiss psychologist.

The Lewinian model

In the 1930s many psychologists took the position that psychological characteristics of individuals were major influences on the person's behaviour. In contrast, Lewin's position was that the group to which an individual belongs is the ground for the individual's perceptions, feelings and actions (Allport, 1948). Thus, the focus of Lewin's work was to construct a scientific system for understanding both the individual and society. He founded the Research Center for Group Dynamics, conducted action research in the social setting and is best known today for his work on group dynamics and motivation.

The major premise of Lewin's work is that behaviour (B) is a function (F) of the person (P) and his or her environment (E). In other words,

B = F(P,E) (Lewin, 1936). Of importance in this equation is that the person (P) and the environment (E) are viewed as mutually dependent upon each other. Understanding the behaviour of an individual in a group setting depends upon understanding both the person's group membership and the person's perceptions.

Research conducted by Lewin and his colleagues on leadership, staff training and conflict resolution led to the identification of concepts that have since been incorporated into experiential learning. For example, individuals who participated in a group discussion were more likely to change their behaviour than those instructed in a lecture. Behavioural changes reported by Lewin (1951) following a group decision-making session (as compared to lecture groups) include greater consumption of fresh milk and mothers giving orange juice to their young babies. The lecture session informed participants of the correct nutritional course of action essential for maintaining good health. In the discussion session about caring for one's family, the participants were viewed as individuals with decision-making ability and the responsibility for guarding their families' health. Information about the benefits of fresh milk and orange juice were not dispensed as doctrine but evolved during the discussions.

Lewin and his colleagues also developed a training programme for leadership and group dynamics that made use of group discussion and joint decision-making. At the end of the day, after the trainees had left, members of the research and training staff shared their observations of the training with each other. One evening, three trainees asked to stay, and their perceptions of the daily events, which differed on occasion from those of the staff, were part of the discussion. The next evening at least half of the trainees attended. The evening session, in which participants shared their perceptions of events, became a significant learning event in the training.

Resolution of an industrial conflict situation also indicated the importance of a three-stage process of resolution. Participants first described their experience from their own perspective followed by addressing the problem in a larger perspective, with assistance. Then group decision-making as to needed changes in policy based on the restated problem concluded the incident (Lewin, 1948).

The situation was a conflict between the supervisor of the sewing machine operators in a factory and the mechanic. The problem involved lost work resulting from machines awaiting repair, an overworked mechanic and the workers' sense of insecurity as to who was the decision-maker on repair problems. The psychologist interviewed the supervisor and the mechanic and, with their permission, assisted the workers in determining a set of priorities for machine repair. These priorities reduced the conflict about which machines were to be repaired first. Requests for the mechanic's assistance (many of which were expressions of the workers' insecurity about repair priorities) also decreased, thus reducing the loss of worker productivity.

From these and other experiences emerged the concepts related to changing behaviour in the social setting. They are concrete experience, observations about the experience, forming new generalizations and concepts about the experience and developing hypotheses and/or policies to address the situation. The hypotheses or policies are then tested through concrete experience and, if necessary, the cycle repeats itself.

Jaques (1985, p 59) describes an adaptation of these concepts in a five-part experiential learning cycle. The five parts are 1) experience; 2) description; 3) interpretation; 4) generalizing; and 5) application. Part 5, application, feeds into experience and the cycle is repeated again. Figure 11.1 describes this cycle.

In summary, the Lewinian model addresses behaviour in interpersonal situations. The model emphasizes the examination and interpretation of concrete experience by the learner. The interpretation, assisted by feedback to the learners, generates new concepts and hypotheses that feed into further concrete experience.

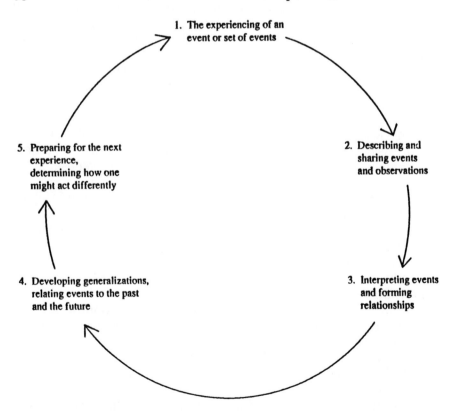

Figure 11.1 *Experiential learning described by Jaques (1985)*

The Piagetian model

During the 1930s a young Swiss psychologist, Jean Piaget, began his studies into the ways that children think. Employed at the Binet Institute, Piaget's task was to develop French versions of questions on English intelligence tests. However, he became intrigued with the reasons children gave for their wrong answers, particularly on the questions that required logical thinking.

From that beginning emerged Piaget's developmental analysis of the growth of intelligence from birth to adulthood (Piaget, 1926; 1972). Intelligence, in his view, is a living system that must adapt to the environment in the same way as a biological organism. That is, it invents or constructs the structures it needs in order to function.

According to Piaget (1972), the learner constructs cognitive structures through two basic processes. One is *assimilation* in which new information is integrated into existing structures (which also enriches the structures). The other is *accommodation*, a process that occurs in two different ways. First, accommodation occurs when the learner's existing cognitive structure is adjusted or modified in order to integrate new information into it. For example, in the industrial situation described earlier, the mechanic and the supervisor adjusted their ways of viewing their roles to accommodate the priority listing of repairs developed by the workers.

Accommodation also occurs at another level. Briefly summarized, it is the reconstruction of a cognitive structure on a higher level of thinking. This process involves the forsaking of intuitive knowledge for logical and more systematic ways of thinking. For example, students are given a problem in which any of several combinations of colourless liquids can change a clear liquid in another beaker to yellow. Individuals who rely on intuitive knowledge will test the possibilities unsystematically, resulting in errors and omissions (Inhelder and Piaget, 1958). In contrast, individuals who address the problem logically first consider all the possible combinations of liquids and make notes about them. They then begin to test the combinations they had devised one by one.

However, reorganizing one's intuitive approaches to problems on a higher level of thinking is not accomplished easily. Three requirements are essential. One is the learner's continued interactions with events in the environment that challenge established perceptions. Another requirement is social interaction with others in which one's beliefs are also challenged. Piaget (1926, p 144) observed that 'never without the shock of contact with the thought of others and the effort of reflection which this shock entails would thought as such come to human consciousness'.

A third requirement is the cognitive conflict (disequilibrium) that is produced by challenges to established perceptions. That is, the person

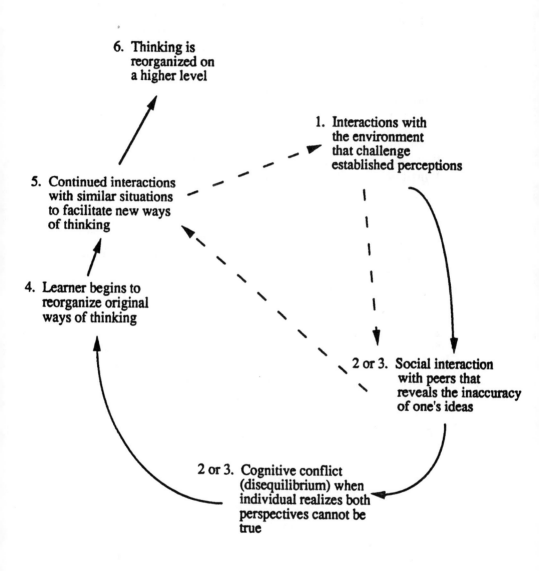

Figure 11.2 *Reorganization of intuitive ways of thinking in the Piagetian model*

realizes that his or her views and the facts or new perceptions that he has just confronted cannot both be true. As a result of this cognitive conflict, the learner begins to reorganize his or her ways of thinking about a particular set of events.

This reorganization, however, does not take place instantly. Investigations conducted by several researchers indicate that several confrontations with one's prior beliefs may be needed for changes to occur (Champagne *et al.*, 1985; Osborne and Gilbert, 1980). Also, adults as well as children experience difficulty in reorganizing their intuitive beliefs (Kuhn and Phelps, 1979).

Figure 11.2 illustrates the phases in the Piagetian model. As indicated, cognitive conflict, which is essential to a reorganization of one's beliefs, may occur as a result of either interactions with the environment or social interactions with peers. Also, note the dashed lines between phases 5, 1 and 2 indicate any needed recycling prior to reorganization of thinking at a more inclusive level.

The sequence of interactions that challenge one's perceptions, social interaction with peers and experiencing cognitive conflict apply to a variety of situations. That is, individuals often develop beliefs about other cultures and ethnic groups based on incomplete or intuitive information. Thus, the Piagetian model is appropriate for reorganizing beliefs or methods of thinking about both physical situations found in nature and social situations embedded in the cultural setting.

Applications

According to the Lewinian model, individuals in a social setting should be led to process their concrete experience in such a way as to arrive at new generalizations and concepts. An important facet of this processing is relating their perceptions of events to larger issues that may require action for a solution. Then the group may develop hypotheses or policies that can be tested by experience. If necessary, the cycle is repeated.

One implication of the Lewinian model is that it is appropriate for situations in which participants experience minor conflict with each other or a team or group is unable to achieve its goals in some way. A post-simulation processing session in which participants share their perceptions of events and their feelings and then work at placing their experiences in a larger framework is essential for learning. Also important, however, are subsequent planned activities in which participants can apply the generalizations and concepts that were developed in the group processing session.

The Piagetian model, in contrast, addresses the situation in which the individual holds inaccurate beliefs and/or implements illogical methods of arriving at conclusions. To begin to change such beliefs and modes of thinking, the individual must be confronted with situations that challenge his or her intuitive knowledge. In other words, the individual must experience cognitive conflict in order to be able to begin to change intuitive conclusions.

An example of a simulation in which the participants experience cognitive conflict is *Me The Slow Learner*. Participants' views of themselves as competent individuals who can overcome obstacles through hard work does not hold true in the simulation. Moreover, they undergo criticism and negative comments from the project staff. Thatcher and Robinson (1990) note that participants often recall earlier school experiences that also were traumatic. In other words, 'many people regress to earlier states when they are confronted with situations similar to those which they lived through and which they thought had been rationalised' (p 267).

PLANNING POST-SIMULATION ACTIVITIES

Typically, the post-simulation activity on which the burden of learning has been placed is the 'debriefing'. The term derives from the use in military exercises and war games when participants, as a group, reviewed and examined the exercise. The participants described events that occurred, accounted for the actions and discussed necessary changes in strategy as indicated by problems encountered during the exercise.

Since the development of war games, simulations have been designed for use at all levels of education in a variety of subject areas and for any of several different purposes. Given such diversity in the nature of the rethinking that is expected to occur, the group processing session can be considered as only one of several post-simulation activities essential to facilitating learning.

Several types of post-simulation activities may be combined to build on the processes set in motion by the simulation. They are the small group or team processing activity, total group sessions, the instructor--student conference, and other specific homework, pair or small-group activities related to the topic.

Small group or team processing

Some simulations, such as *In the Hot Seat*, involve a single team facing a particular problem or issue. Participants take roles in the simulation with particular responsibilities; however, individual efforts must also be coordinated to produce the final outcome. Alternative strategies may be explored in the post-simulation group session. However, discussion should not drift into recriminations of individual team members.

Other simulations are designed in which participants take roles in different teams. In some data-management simulations, teams are managing different banks, businesses or other ventures during the exercise. In these exercises, the facilitator may make use of a small group debriefing prior to a total group session. Two advantages of the small group activity are given by Pearson and Smith (1986, p 167). First, it provides the team members an opportunity to consider the goals they established and their strategies prior to interacting in the large group.

Second, issues arising from interpersonal actions that may precipitate conflict or anger in members of other teams can be addressed beforehand in the small group. Simulations in which two groups are competing for the same goal are one example. Others are exercises in which one group's task is to deliver services to others, such as social workers and their clients.

The disadvantage of the small group interaction is that the perceptions of the group members may solidify toward other teams or their participants (Pearson and Smith, 1986). This potential problem may be countered in at least three ways. First, the team debriefing should be short, for example, limited to 15 minutes. Second, the team debriefing should be conducted for specific goals. For example, team members may be directed to review briefly the objectives they established in the exercise and their strategies. Or they may be asked to consider briefly alternative ways to achieve their goals for any of their strategies that may have generated conflict or anger in others during the simulation. A third suggestion offered by Pearson and Smith (1986) is to arrange the seating in the whole group activity so that members from different teams are interspersed with each other.

The whole group processing session

The total group activity, often referred to as 'debriefing', is appropriate for initiating learning following any multiple-participant simulation. Depending on the nature of the simulation, the group processing session may address either of two general purposes. One is the development of generalizations from the interpretation of learner perceptions (the Lewinian model). The other is that of beginning to address the cognitive conflict that has arisen from challenges to the learners' intuitive beliefs or methods of thinking (the Piagetian model).

When implemented with tactical-decision simulations, the group processing session addresses the learners' interpretation of their perspectives that led them to select particular goals and/or strategies. That is, teams in tactical-decision simulations are attempting to solve complex problems as a group in their assigned roles. Therefore, one purpose of the group session is the analysis of the data selection, interpretation and/or the management strategies of the participants. The participants first describe their perceptions of events and then address the perspectives that led to a particular course of action. They also may examine alternative organizational strategies or decisions that might have been implemented. For instance, company officials reconsider ways they may have improved profitability, customer service and other goals established during the simulation.

The group session following a language skills/communication simulation also focuses on the participants' efforts to accomplish their goals. This learning is initiated in the group session in which participants explore alternative ways to communicate a particular idea, the points at which they missed important information conveyed by others and related issues.

Minor conflicts may also arise in tactical-decision and language skills simulations that require processing. In such situations, the group session should address their perceptions and relate those perceptions to a larger issue, such as incomplete data, need for improved communication and so on. Pearson and Smith (1986, p 159) note that even an innocuous group activity may trigger expressions of anger and conflict. They describe a student teacher's violent outburst at hearing other students' accounts of their practice teaching experiences. She viewed their experiences as far more positive than her own and reacted negatively to their reports.

Social-process simulations, however, because they focus on inter-personal activities, are the exercises most likely to generate emotional reactions.

Following *The Numbers Game*, for instance, participants must face their inadequate attempts to address a cooperative learning situation. In *Talking Rocks*, some groups may become hostile toward other groups who left uninterpretable messages which resulted in the 'death' of the receivers during the simulation. An initial generalization that may evolve from the group session is that while some of the Eagle people died, the good messages left by some groups helped others in the tribe to improve their skills (Jones, 1982, p 68).

When a simulation produces high levels of cognitive conflict, however, the group session is only a first step in the students' reorganization of their beliefs on a higher level. Because participants often continue to process the events for days and weeks after the exercise (Thatcher and Robinson, 1990), a series of activities following the simulation is essential.

Leading the whole group session

Three major phases, derived from the Lewinian model, are typically included in the group session for social-process simulations. They are a) to determine the events that occurred; b) to identify participants' thoughts and feelings about the events; and c) to develop initial generalizations based on the experience.

Given the multiple concerns to be addressed in the group, it is particularly important that the leader allows adequate time for the session. The time should be sufficient for as much exploration as individuals are able to undertake. At a minimum, the activity should be scheduled for the same amount of time as that allocated to the simulation itself (Pearson and Smith, 1986).

The instructor who is leading the group activity is not serving as the holder of expert knowledge. Instead, the role is that of facilitator in assisting the participants to process the events of the simulation, their feelings and to begin to move toward relating of their experience to larger issues. Thus, the leader is not functioning in the role of judge or jury. Instead, he or she must be sensitive to the messages conveyed by participants' comments in order to raise thoughtful questions for their consideration at the appropriate time.

Determining the simulation events

The purpose for beginning with participants' descriptions of events is twofold. First, it is a non-threatening issue and second, it provides a common starting point for all participants (Pearson and Smith, 1986, p 159). Moreover, since individuals perceive events in different ways, they are likely to report events differently. The reporting, therefore, permits all participants to acquire a basic knowledge of the experiences of the others (Pearson and Smith, 1986).

As already described in Chapter 10, sessions following simulations that generate high levels of cognitive conflict should take a somewhat different approach. Participant completion of a questionnaire that addresses both events and emotions followed by immediate comments are suggested by Thatcher and Robinson (1990). Given the intensity of participants' experiences during the exercise, this strategy assists them to 'let off steam' and to begin the transition toward discussing the exercise in more detail.

For simulations that are less intense experiences for the group, participants can begin to share events as they perceive them with the others. Some suggestions for group leaders by van Ments (1983) are helpful. First, the purpose of this phase of processing is descriptive, not evaluative. In addition, the leader should use open-ended questions (how? and what?) to initiate comments. Actions that were taken rather than actions that might have been taken should be the focus. Also, quality of performance is not evaluated, motives or judgements about underlying attitudes are not made and any feedback should be in the form of the individual's own experience rather than that of another participant (van Ments, 1983).

The leader should also be alert to identifying the individuals who have little to say or who volunteer only perfunctory remarks. They may hold quite different views of the experience from those expressed by the others. Depending on the level of trust that has been established, they may share their feelings and views in one or more conferences with the instructor.

Identifying participants' feelings
This phase of processing is crucial to any redirection and reorganization of thinking that may occur and it should not be conducted in a superficial manner. Essential to the success of this phase is an atmosphere of trust, an acceptance of others and a feeling of safety that promotes participants' willingness to take risks (Pearson and Smith, 1986, p 159).

For example, some groups in *Talking Rocks* may be upset by one or more of the other groups because they left vague or incomprehensible messages. Therefore, the climate in the group session must be such that the participants are comfortable in expressing their frustration and anger about that development.

Important skills for the group leader are a sensitivity to the underlying emotions of the participants and skills in handling interpersonal anger and conflict (Pearson and Smith, 1986, p 159). The leader must not be judgemental and he or she must refrain from reinterpreting participants' statements by paraphrasing or summarizing. Instead, the leader must be sensitive to participants' concerns and direct the discussion toward addressing those concerns (Pearson and Smith, 1986).

Developing initial generalizations
This phase of the processing, like the identification of participant emotions and concerns, is critical to the learning. For simulations that do not generate high levels of cognitive conflict, a few generalizations may be formed during this phase of the group session. Once participants' feelings and concerns are addressed, the processing can begin to deal with events or actions in the simulation that were not consistent with prior viewpoints, popular beliefs or theories. Thus, the processing begins to address events or actions in the simulation that resulted from different views of a situation. At this point, the leader's role is to encourage discussions in this direction and to raise questions that bring discrepancies to the attention of the participants. Once discrepancies are identified, students may begin to extend their thinking to a broader context.

The instructor-student conference

The instructor-student conference plays an important role in facilitating learning after the simulation. However, it is implemented in somewhat different ways for single-participant and group simulations.

The single participant simulation
The purpose of single participant simulations is to develop students'

problem-solving skills. Students may be diagnosing a particular problem, managing a data set, or interviewing a client, witness or patient. The instructor–student conference is the primary mechanism for analysing the student's experience.

The instructor in this situation is fulfilling a dual role. First, he or she is functioning in part as the holder of expert knowledge (Pearson and Smith, 1986). Second, the instructor is a facilitator for the participant in analysing his or her own performance and particular strengths and weaknesses.

The conference should include at least three major stages. The first is to determine the student's perception of his or her performance during the exercise and some general assessment of strengths and weaknesses. The second is to discuss the student's decisions at each point in the exercise as a way of reconciling the student's perceptions with the performance data. That is, errors in deducing outcomes from the data indicators and errors in relating diagnoses of the problem or data reports on the participant's manipulation of variables to appropriate management steps are also discussed. Minor misconceptions that can be addressed in the conference are also corrected. The third and concluding phase is the selection of follow-up activities for the student.

For diagnostic simulations, the process standard for the conference is the optimal route through the simulation that was identified when the map of the exercise was developed (recall Figure 5.1). The computer program of the simulation maintains a record of the student's chosen options (essential, facilitative, neutral, impeding, harmful). Thus, the instructor has a profile of the student's strategy throughout the exercise. This information is important because some students may make the right diagnosis and select an appropriate course of action in an efficient and effective way. Others, however, may stumble into it by using the 'scattergun approach'. That is, the student may choose several options at each decision point, thus compensating for a lack of knowledge. The computer record of the student's decisions assists the instructor in clearly differentiating the performance of the student who has made only a few miscalculations from the one who has floundered through the decision-making.

Depending on the nature of the errors, the student may be assigned specific reading materials and/or to work through problem-solving exercises specifically designed to improve the student's cognitive strategies. Such exercises, unlike diagnostic simulations, alert the student when he or she has made a major tactical error. The program then routes the student through the decision point again and notes the nature of the error. Profiles developed from these exercises indicate the number of times the program redirected the student at each decision point. If needed, further remediation can be planned following these exercises.

Capabilities that are important in interviewing simulations include both cognitive and affective skills. That is, in addition to astutely eliciting information, the interviewer must gain the confidence of the interviewee in order to be successful.

As mentioned in Chapter 9, the interview is videotaped. The conference should begin with student concerns, since the student may express some anxiety about the exercise. Then the conference can move to more general issues, addressing the specifics in the instructor's notes. Following the conference with the instructor, the 'client' or 'patient' also often provides feedback to the student on his or her particular feelings, degree of confidence in the interviewer and other observations.

When used as a part of professional training, diagnostic and interviewing simulations are often implemented on a continuing basis. Thus, students have many opportunities over a term or a year to improve their skills. Also, as the student gains proficiency, the simulations may become more difficult. For example, the interviewing simulations may begin with simple cases and fairly cooperative 'patients' or 'clients'. Later exercises, however, may address difficult cases and recalcitrant and/or forgetful 'witnesses' or 'clients'. When single participant simulations are implemented in a progressively more difficult series, later instructor–student conferences address cumulative progress as well as the level of cognitive and affective skills demonstrated by the student.

The group simulation

Of primary importance in planning post-simulation activities is that it is the *individual* who experiences the simulation, not the group. A common danger in the use of simulations is to see only the group and to fail to determine the nature of the individual's experience (Vernon, 1990, p 241). Yet, each student develops a separate understanding and interpretation of the simulation. Moreover, even well-developed and reliable materials may generate covert and unanticipated messages (Vernon, 1990, p 240). Therefore, instructor–student conferences are essential in addition to the group session for at least two reasons. One is that the one-to-one conference is an important mechanism in the detection of spurious learnings.

Another major purpose of the conference is to allow participants to express thoughts and feelings that may not have been processed during the group session. The role of the instructor in this situation is that of facilitator. That is, the instructor assists the student in clarifying his or her views and emotions and in arriving at some resolution of conflicting ideas or feelings. However, the instructor is not a professional counsellor. If the student seems unable to let go of the experience or continues to be disturbed by it in some way, the school psychologist or school counsellor should be informed.

Other post-simulation activities

A key component of the Lewinian experiential model is the opportunity to test in practice the new generalizations that evolved from the concrete experience. Also, according to the Piagetian model, as individuals begin to reorganize their thinking on a higher level, continued interactions with similar situations and opportunities to continue rethinking the experience are needed.

Therefore, group and individual activities are essential following the initial processing session. As already indicated, the goals of single participant simulations and group tactical-decision simulations are, for the most, the development of students' cognitive strategies. Therefore, these simulations are typically followed by specific home-work and in-class activities that address thinking and organizational strategies in similar situations.

Follow-up activities to the social-process simulation should include some combination of large-group and small-group discussions, two-person collaborative assignments and individual homework assignments that build on the concepts developed in the simulation. The purpose is to allow continued verbalizations about the simulation with feedback from peers. Vernon (1990, p 241) notes that when participants leave a simulation experience with one follow-up session, they are never again a part of the same group that shared the experience. In such situations, opportunities to continue processing the experience are lost.

Developing or selecting specific follow-up activities to the group session for social-system simulations, such as *The Numbers Game*, *Talking Rocks* and *St Philip*, implies that the simulation itself was selected for some purpose that would precipitate critical thinking. That is, the simulation is implemented for a more specific purpose than that of simply developing general vague realizations, eg, issues are more complex than they appear on the surface.

For example, the group session may lead to the generalization that the particular simulation is an analogy for some other experience. One such exercise is the simulation *Talking Rocks* which challenges the idea that primitive societies are unsophisticated and composed of 'ignorant' people. The exercise confronts the participants with the ingenuity required to overcome adverse situations when tools that others take for granted are missing. Subsequent class activities may address other social situations in which individuals have great difficulty in succeeding because they lack the appropriate tools or skills.

Similarly, in *The Numbers Game*, participants expect an instructor-managed, non-collaborative situation. Typically, several minutes pass before participants address the task as it is presented. Subsequent activities, therefore, may explore other group situations in which mistaken assumptions thwart positive action. Participants in *St Philip*, on the other hand, may read news stories in which communities are debating the advantages and disadvantages of an intrusive industry or are organizing to fight a development viewed as harmful.

Empathy/insight simulations, as indicated in Chapter 10, may generate high levels of cognitive conflict. As indicated by the Piagetian model, resolution of such conflict through new ways of thinking is an extended process. Such simulations should be followed by two group sessions, one of which takes place after a short break at the end of the simulation. The other should be scheduled a week or so later to allow participants on their own and informally with each other to further process the events.

Also, at least one instructor–student conference is a must for the empathy/insight exercise. The intensity of the emotions that are generated and the loss of esteem that may occur, however temporary, can affect the learner for an extended period of time. In addition, traumatic events often lead to the recall of memories for similar events in one's life that the student may not be ready to share with his or her peers. Thus, an instructor–student conference in which the student has the opportunity to discuss the experience further is essential.

In addition to the activities suggested in Chapter 10, other activities may address the general climate important for empathetic decision-making. For example, participants in *Me The Slow Learner* may visit different schools and informally observe the climate established by the administration for the degree of emphasis placed on meeting different student needs.

Another useful activity is that of students each maintaining a journal in which they jot down thoughts and impressions about their experiences. Students may share some of these thoughts with others in small group discussions if they wish.

An important characteristic of simulations is that different administrations will generate different actions, thoughts and feelings because individuals react in different ways to the same open-ended situation. Administrators, therefore, must guard against expecting the same reactions in subsequent implementations of the same simulation. As Lewin indicated, behaviour is a function of the person and the environment: $B = F(P, E)$.

In summary, simulations can be powerful learning experiences. However, they must be carefully selected and implementation should include all the components in the related experiential model.

EVALUATING POST-SIMULATION ACTIVITIES

Single-participant simulations

Step 1: Review the instructor–student conference.
  • Did the conference focus on the participant's task in the

 simulation (data-management, diagnosis, language/communication)?
- Were the student's strategy and content errors addressed?
- Were the student's strengths also emphasized in the simulation?
- Were three phases included in the conference (establishing student perceptions, reviewing student strategies, identifying appropriate follow-up activities for the student)?

Step 2: Review follow-up assignments.
- Is independent research on major concepts appropriate, given the tasks in the simulation?
- Are practice exercises similar to difficult components of the simulation available?
- Are related readings and sample case studies available that are keyed to concepts and skills expected in the simulation?
- Are activities available that provide further opportunities for students to implement new skills demonstrated in the simulation?

Team simulations

Step 1: Analyse the group post-simulation discussion.
- Did the discussion move from participant perceptions of events to the examination of alternative courses of action?
- Was the facilitator prepared for minor conflicts among team members that may occur?
- What sources of evidence or verbal cues critical to implementing effective strategies in the simulation were identified in the post-simulation discussion?
- Did the discussion address the ways that the team members may coordinate their efforts more effectively in the future?
- Was sufficient time allowed for team members to contribute to the discussion and to process the information?

Step 2: Review follow-up activities.
- See single-participant simulations.
- Are cooperative activities for 2–3 participants available?

Large-group simulations

Step 1: Determine the appropriate experiential model for the simulation and the post-simulation activities.
- Is the expected process that of beginning to develop new generalizations (Lewinian model)?
- Is the simulation designed to challenge participants' accepted beliefs, ie, create cognitive conflict or disequilibrium (the Piagetian model)?

The Lewinian Model

Step 2: Analyse the post-simulation discussion.
- Was the allocated time at least equal to the time spent in the simulation?
- Were three broad stages included (participant perceptions of events, identification of participants' thoughts and feelings, initial efforts to develop generalizations)?
- Were open-ended questions (How? What?) used to elicit student perceptions?
- What new generalizations evolved from the discussion?
- Did all participants have ample opportunity to express their thoughts and feelings?

Step 3: Review follow-up activities.
- See step 1 of team simulations.
- What subsequent small-group or large-group activities are available that permit participants to test their new generalizations?

The Piagetian Model

Step 2: Analyse the initial large-group discussion.
- Was a brief coffee break included between the end of the simulation and the large-group discussion?
- Was a brief questionnaire that addresses both events and emotions used at the beginning of the large-group session?
- Was the time allocated to the large-group session at least as long as the simulation?
- Did the initial discussion primarily focus on the emotions generated by the cognitive conflict in the simulation (participant confusion, frustration and other negative emotions)?
- Did the initial discussion also explore the significance of different kinds of behaviours in the simulation, such as giggling and mild aggression?
- Did all participants have an ample opportunity to express their thoughts and feelings?

Step 3: Review the sequence of follow-up activities.
- Is at least one instructor–student conference scheduled in 10–14 days?
- Was a second large-group discussion scheduled in approximately 14–21 days?
- Are activities scheduled for pairs or teams of students to explore similar or related situations?
- Are related topics and analogous situations provided in related readings?
- Are small-group activities planned in which students have

> an opportunity to discuss and/or execute different strategies that may develop as a result of the simulation experience?
> - Is maintaining a journal appropriate for the next few weeks for students?
> - Is the second large-group session planned to assist students in reorganizing their thinking on a higher level?
> - What subsequent thoughts and observations are expressed by participants?
> - In what ways can students' reorganization of thinking interact with subsequent topics in the course or workshop?

REFERENCES

Allport, G (1948) 'Foreword', in Lewin, K, *Resolving Social Conflicts: Selected Papers on Group Dynamics*, iii–ix, London: Harper & Row.

Champagne, A B, Gunstone, R F and Klopfer, L E (1985) 'Effecting changes in cognitive structures among physics students', in West, L H J and Pine, A L (eds) *Cognitive Structure and Conceptual Changes*, 163–88, Orlando, FL: Academic Press.

Inhelder, B and Piaget, J (1958) *The Growth of Logical Thinking from Childhood to Adolescence*, New York: Basic Books.

Jaques, D (1985) 'Debriefing, debriefing', in van Ments, M and Hearndon, K (eds) *Effective Use of Games and Simulations*, 55–66, Loughborough: SAGSET, Loughborough Institute of Technology.

Jones, K (1982) *Simulations in Language Learning*, Cambridge: Cambridge University Press.

Kuhn, D and Phelps, E (1979) 'A methodology for observing development of a formal reasoning strategy', *New Directions for Child Development*, **5**, 45–57.

Lewin, K (1936) *Principles of Topological Psychology*, New York: McGraw-Hill.

Lewin, K (1948) 'The solving of a chronic conflict in industry', in Lewin, K *Resolving Social Conflicts: Selected Papers on Group Dynamics*, New York: Harper & Row.

Lewin, K (1951) *Field Theory in Social Science*, New York: Harper & Row.

Osborne, R J and Gilbert, J K (1980) 'A technique for exploring students' views of the world', *Physics Education*, **15**, 376–9.

Pearson, M and Smith, D (1986) 'Debriefing in experience-based learning', *Simulation/Games for Learning*, **16**, 4, 155–72.

Piaget, J (1926) *Judgment and Reasoning in the Child*, New York: Harcourt.

Piaget, J (1970) *Science of Education and the Psychology of the Child*, New York: Orion.

Piaget, J (1972) *The Principles of Genetic Epistemology*, New York: Basic Books.

Piaget, J (1973) *To Understand is to Invent: The Future of Education*, New York: Grossman.

Thatcher, D and Robinson, J (1990) 'Me The Slow Learner – a case study', *Simulation/Games for Learning*, **13**, 1, 10–16.

van Ments, M (1983) *The Effective Use of Role Play. A Handbook for Teachers and Trainers*, London: Kogan Page.
Vernon, L (1990) 'Ethical issues', in Crookall, D and Oxford, R L (eds), *Simulation, Gaming and Language*, New York: Newbury House.

12 Other interactive exercises

Experiential learning is a broad category that includes a variety of learning activities. Simulations, as indicated in the prior chapter, include a large group of interactive learning experiences that are characterized by two major features. First, the participants take on clearly differentiated functional roles with associated responsibilities, consequences and privileges. Second, in executing those roles, they either interact with others in efforts to achieve particular goals or interact with a complex evolving problem or task.

Other types of experiential learning activities are sometimes confused with simulations. These other activities have one or the other of the key characteristics of simulations, but not both. In role play exercises and microworlds, for example, participants take on loosely defined roles that they can often shape in different ways. In contrast, group problem-solving activities with simulated materials or in simulated settings provide experience with a complex problem. However, students do not interact with the problem in a functional role capacity. Instead, students remain, for the most part, on the outside of the hypothetical situation instead of operating from the inside as in a simulation.

ROLE PLAY AND MICROWORLDS

Both role play and microworlds are interactive exercises in which students take different roles. However, they differ in a number of characteristics. Both activities are useful in a variety of classroom settings.

Role play

One activity that may be confused with simulations is that of role play. Although both exercises involve participants taking on particular roles, several differences may be identified. Perhaps the most important difference is that the simulation is a complex, evolving exercise and a role play is a single incident. That is, a role play may involve a situation such as a school psychologist dealing with an angry parent or a customer returning a defective item to a shop, and so on. As a result of the specificity of the incident or task, role plays are typically short exercises of 10 to 20 minutes. A simulation, in contrast, may run from

40 minutes in several days, depending on the nature of the exercise.

Unlike role plays, participants in a simulation are provided with a variety of information that includes goals, objectives, constraints and background information. The participant accepts his or her responsibilities as a prime minister, space ship captain, teacher or bone expert on an archaeological team. The participant executes a particular set of responsibilities within assigned parameters, using the facts provided. In other words, participants do not invent background information or improvise facts or events. Instead, they execute a particular set of responsibilities using given information.

In contrast, the participants in a role play do not receive detailed background information. Instead, they receive a brief outline of the situation and sketchy information about the role. Directions, for instance, may read, 'You are an angry parent who is upset because your son is not doing well in school'. Thus, the individual is free to improvise events and reactions compatible with the brief role description.

The instructor in a foreign language class, for instance, may set up a situation in which one student is a visitor to Paris who is hungry and has just entered a restaurant. Another student is the waiter. The two students improvise their verbal exchange as the visitor sets about ordering something to eat and drink.

In contrast, the simulation *Space Crash*, also used in foreign language classrooms, is an exercise with a complex task that specifies the types of actions to be taken (those that lead to survival) and role cards that must be addressed. The participants must integrate their separate sources of information in order to survive. Improvisation or invention is not only implausible, it is counter-productive to the goal of the simulation.

Role play may be used for any of several purposes: to practise a particular skill, to explore a particular area of a subject more deeply, or to sensitize students to the feelings of others (van Ments, 1984). Also, the role play may be set in the present, the future or in some past historical period. That is, the participants may take the roles of well-known literary or historical figures and address a particular issue.

One feature of simulations is that there are no observers. In contrast, because role plays involve so few persons, they often take place in a 'fishbowl' setting (van Ments, 1983). That is, the remainder of the class serves as observers. This arrangement places additional strain on the students in the role play. An alternative suggested by van Ments (1983) is the 'multiple' technique. The class is divided into small groups and each group runs its own role play. Each group may also identify one person as an observer who reports to the plenary session after the activity.

When the role involves conflict or some mental transformation is required to enact the role, debriefing should be conducted after the role play. This provides the individuals an opportunity to get out of the role at the conclusion of the exercise. Van Ments (1984) suggests that informal questions should be used to elicit the feelings of the individuals during the exercise. A question that might be asked of the person in the role of school psychologist is, 'How did you feel about the parent's accusation that you weren't doing your job?'

After the individuals have an opportunity to discuss their feelings and any false impressions that may have arisen, then observers may be invited to comment (van Ments, 1984). The final stage is that of analysis. At this point, the role players should be able to comment objectively on the exercise along with the observers.

Although traditionally associated with oral performance, role plays may be adapted for use in other forms. One application is written activities. Scarcella and Stern (1990) describe the use of dramatic monologues for reading and writing skills. In the monologue, the student selects a character from a literary work and assumes the role of that character. The student then writes the character's reactions to a particular situation, issue or other character. For example, Biff in Arthur Miller's *Death of a Salesman* could explain exactly what he meant when he said, 'Pop, I'm a dime a dozen, and so are you' (Scarcella and Stern, 1990, p 123).

The spontaneity of the interactive role play is, of course, missing from such exercises. However, the students gain practice in using their reading and writing skills for specific goals related to another setting, time and place.

Another application makes use of computer managed interactive videodisc technology. The Target Interactive Project *Tip-Dart*, designed for adolescents, explores situations in which substance abuse occurs. The exercise takes place at a party and asks the viewers to make critical decisions about drugs and alcohol that adolescents have to make (Barlow, 1990 p 15). (Target, the developer of *Tip-Dart*, is a non-profit service organization of the National Association of State High Schools, USA and IBM Educational Systems).

One purpose of the project is to teach adolescents ways to refuse potentially dangerous substances without losing status in the eyes of their peers and to prepare them for uncomfortable situations (Barlow, 1990, p 15). Students choose which of nine teenage characters they wish to be and make all the decisions for that character in a dramatized party situation. Although professional actors are playing out the actions of the teenagers on the screen, the students c y see the consequences of the decisions they have selected for their characters.

The situation begins when Cathy's parents go out for the evening, leaving Cathy responsible for her younger brother. A few minutes later, a group of teenage 'friends' drop in 'to keep her company and party' (Barlow, 1990, p 15). Soon the teenagers are offered alcohol and other types of drugs in a series of incidents. Viewers make decisions using IBM's Info Window touch screen technology and then view the outcomes of the decisions. One set of decisions, for example, is whether to allow a friend to take another drink, to use drugs or to drive drunk. On-screen symbols permit the viewer to repeat a particular sequence, to move ahead to another scene, or to stop the program, in addition to making decisions for their character.

An evaluation of *Tip-Dart* involved 24 male and 24 female students who responded to a written questionnaire about their perceptions of the materials (Leone, 1990). Respondents preferred viewing the dramatization alone or with a few class mates rather than in a classroom situation. They considered the party situation to be similar to real life situations they had experienced. Additional material suggested by the students included involving the police and the law as a consequence of substance abuse and following the characters after they leave the party (Leone, 1990, p 17).

The students are not directly experiencing the effects of their decisions as they would in a 'live' role play. However, the topic of substance abuse, like other issues that adolescents face, is inextricably linked to their self-images and relations with their peers. Thus, the party situation, since it appears to be presented in a realistic manner, is appropriate for the videodisc exercise.

Microworlds

The term *microworld* refers to computer-based materials that establish particular environments or settings for student activity. Ideally, a microworld places the student into another world in which he or she experiences aspects of life as others experience it. In other words, the materials do not simply simulate a particular setting; they also involve the students in an active way in events, problems and issues reflective of a particular setting and/or time. Like a role play, the microworld should permit students to behave as themselves within the constraints and characteristics of a particular setting and role.

One method of developing microworlds makes use of the database capability of the microcomputer and a 'movement-simulator' based on the adventure-game model (Martin, 1985, p 205). The movement-simulator provides a framework of travel and incident, and the developed databases include a large collection of ancillary information.

One project, *Scotland 100 Years Ago*, was designed for primary classrooms. The class is divided into six groups and each group takes the role of a fictitious character. The authentic characters reflect different levels of social standing of the times. They range from Victoria Alice Stewart-Forbes, an aristocrat, to James Gordon, a clerk and Jean Muir, a labourer's widow (Martin, 1985).

Each group receives a scenario that requires their character to make a journey across Scotland. After the group plans the journey for their character, the actual movement is determined by the computer (using the movement-simulator). Because the movement in any one session is restricted, frequent pauses occur during the journey. Authentic incidents involving the characters also take place and the characters may acquire and lose worldly possessions (Martin, 1985).

During the pauses in the journey, each group may engage in any of a variety of activities which may be creative, descriptive, dramatic or investigative. Possibilities include 'mapwork, creative writing (diaries, newspaper reports, descriptions), drama (plays, taped interviews with characters), historical and geographical research and the presentation of findings, and art and craft work (drawings of scenes and situations, friezes, models)' (Martin, 1985, p 203).

One key to the success of such a project is the quality and extent of material in the supporting database. Two databases were developed for *Scotland 100 Years Ago.* Database 1 contains passages of information. For example, one item is an entry from 'The Diary of Mary Bell' (April 9, 1883) in which the 15-year-old writes she has just lost her job as a housemaid. She speculates on the reasons why the Rev. Burns fired her. Another is from 'Incidents Which May Have Occurred Whilst Journeying 100 Years ago' that describes the robbery experienced by Callum McPherson, the lawyer who is travelling on foot.

Database 2 contains a list of information sources, 30 photographs, story-sheets with details of the characters and other documents. In addition to the databases, ancillary materials include handbooks, maps, facsimiles of documents and pictures.

At each pause in the journey, each group decides on an activity it wishes to complete. Thus an important feature of the project is the group interaction and cooperation (Martin, 1985). That is, the group plans each activity using the talents and interests of the group, then allocates and executes the necessary tasks.

The structure of these activities reflects an important purpose for education described by Dewey (1916). That is, the emphasis in instruction should be on personal experimentation, planning and reinvention by the child, since the goal of the curriculum is the development of social power and insight.

Consider the differences between *Scotland 100 Years Ago* and *The Irish Immigrant Experience* described in Chapter 7. *The Irish Immigrant Experience* provides a limited database of economic factors that students are to manipulate. Also, although the students take the names of actual passengers who arrived in Boston in 1859, the role carries no significance other than that the passenger is poor. Some may be more likely to find work than others, but the role per se does not pervade the student's experience unless the teacher selects or develops additional activities or materials.

Moreover, manipulating the set of variables and planning the next course of action depends on interaction with the microcomputer. However, only one student from the group can interact with the computer at one time and often groups must wait to take their turn. Finally, although the groups are encouraged to make entries into diaries for their particular character, the purpose is to learn to use the text-processing capability of Appleworks. Thus, the activity adds little to learning about the experiences of poor Irish immigrants.

In contrast, *Scotland 100 Years Ago* functions as a rich resource of information that students then pursue on their own. In addition, the six roles form a unifying thread throughout the curriculum. They are represented in the passage entries and incidents that occur. Their difficulties and problems, most of which evolve from their status in life, provide various opportunities for students to understand life in another century as they identify with their characters. Thus the role has meaning beyond that of simply serving as the mechanism to 'jump start' the lesson.

Second, the computer is not the centre of learning; it is an adjunct. Students learn to access the databases and then consult the recommended sources or build on the incidents in their own way. Thus, the time spent on the computer is short, since most of the activity occurs elsewhere. Also important is that the materials produced by the computer, such as text passages, instruction, maps and so on may be printed out and taken to the work centres (Martin, 1985).

In summary, a properly designed microworld frees both the teacher and the student to be creative. It provides a framework for a variety of different kinds of learning acquired in a cooperative rather than a competitive setting.

PROBLEM-SOLVING WITH SIMULATED MATERIALS

Simulations are problem-based exercises set in a particular context in which the participant is assigned a well-designed credible role. The participant as problem-solver is, therefore, functioning as an integral component of the context in which the problem arises and develops. In other words, the problem-solver is on the inside of the situation.

The key to the experience for the participant is that of being a defined, functional and essential component of the ongoing situation. As a result, both the problem and the participant are influenced by the experience. For example, in diagnostic, crisis-management and data-management simulations, the data selected by the participant influences the way that the problem or task unfolds for the participants. In other words, participants or teams that select or discover different data indicators face different problems.

In contrast, some problem-solving exercises make use of simulated materials or settings, but the problem-solvers are not functional elements within the situation. They face a complex yet finite task (or series of tasks) that does not change or evolve in response to their decisions or actions. In other words, the problem-solver is not an integral element that functions within the problem and its context.

Use of print materials

Problem solving using print materials of simulated situations may be either individual or group activities. One example, appropriate for individual students or pairs of students, is the 'Humber Bridge exercise' (Dalton *et al.*, 1972). The basis for the exercise is three maps of Lincolnshire and Yorkshire. The first task is to mark on map 1 a) the shortest current route between Lincoln and Hull and b) the shortest possible route when the bridge is built. Then using the scale of 2 cm : 5 km, the student measures the present and future distances and the number of kilometres saved by the bridge. Using a chart of estimated current distances between other towns in the area, the student enters the distance between each town and Hull in the spaces provided on the map. The student then draws lines to enclose the towns that are 15, 30, 45 and 60 km from Hull. The same decisions are made about future distances using map 2. The student then compares the two maps. Finally, the student consults map 1 again and determines the total urban population at present, after the bridge is built and the differences between them.

Group problem-solving exercises with simulated materials often involve issues in which teams can take different positions. They develop their argument and then defend their decisions to the others. In fact, issues that form the basis for social-system simulations may be developed instead as group problem-solving exercises. For example, the map and background information for *St Philip* may be presented to two groups of students, each of which is assigned a position on the building of the tourist hotel on the island. Each group develops its rationale and defends its stand before a panel of judges (other students) selected in advance.

The major difference between such exercises and the simulation is the assignment of different roles and the reality of function experienced by participants as they execute the responsibilities and privileges of the assigned role. The group problem-solving format may be used in classes in which working in teams and developing a team position is an important classroom goal. The simulation, on the other hand, may be used when one of the goals is to experience the difficulty of negotiating and resolving issues in elected decision-making bodies.

Use of videodisc technology

Computer-managed videodiscs are useful instructional devices that combine the imaging of film and television with the branching capability of the computer. As indicated in Chapters 6 and 9, computer-managed videodiscs may be used to develop simulations in which the reactions to participant decisions are live-action images. Videodisc technology is also being used to develop other types of problem-solving activities. At present, interactive videodisc projects have been completed for various kinds of problem solving. Two types are troubleshooting and maintaining complex equipment and providing 'dry lab' experiments in science courses.

Troubleshooting complex equipment

The Air Training Command of the US Air Force uses a wide variety of media to create training environments that closely resemble the situations in which the graduate trainee is expected to perform. The media include part-task trainers, static displays, equipment trainers and computer-based instruction.

In the late 1980s, the Air Training Command began testing the application of interactive videodisc technology to selected training problems. The initial application involved maintenance training on the AN/GPN-22 Precision Approach Radar, a sensitive and complex system used in the control of aircraft (Clark, 1988, p 32). The completed videodisc contains approximately 80 000 still frames. Among them are the removal of major and minor components, switch manipulation, test equipment hookups, component adjustments and many other maintenance actions. The tasks span approximately 200 hours of performance training. The tasks range in complexity from the location of major subassemblies to complete alignment of the transmitter and receiver (Clark, 1988, p 33).

The interactive videodisc technology is used as an alternative to training on actual equipment in maintenance courses. Trainees may accomplish each task in a demonstration, practice or test mode and repeat each task until mastery is achieved. Computer-generated prompts assist the trainee in the demonstration mode whereas the trainee may use only the required maintenance manuals in the practice mode. The only difference between the practice and test modes is that the trainee's performance is automatically scored in the latter (Clark, 1988, p 33). Preliminary findings indicated that the interactive videodisc costs are approximately one-twelfth of the costs of a three-dimensional simulator and the training is as effective.

Providing 'dry labs' in science

Videodisc technology is particularly useful for the development of 'dry lab' experiments in chemistry, physics and biology courses which include laboratory sessions in the curriculum.

A development created in the chemistry department at the University of Illinois at Champagne–Urbana, USA, includes 30 lessons on chemical reactions, solubility, gases and kinetics and equilibrium (Smith and Jones, 1989). Some of the lessons supplement the laboratory experiments and others prepare students to perform procedures they will use in the laboratory later. The lessons are used by approximately 3 000 students a year in a learning centre equipped with 39 networked microcomputers with laser disc players. The introductory chemistry course alternates weeks of laboratory experiments with the self-paced lessons in the learning centre.

Some systems that use the microcomputer to control the videodisc player display the images on a conventional television monitor and computer-generated text appears on the computer screen. The Illinois project, in contrast, uses a single screen system in which computer text and graphics are superimposed on video images (Smith and Jones, 1986).

Several advantages of the technology were identified by the developers. First, students can experiment with reactions that are too dangerous or not possible in the laboratory setting. An example is the dust-explosion experiment in which dust is pumped into a transparent model of a grain elevator which contains a spark generator (Smith and Jones, 1986).

Second, students can conduct a greater number of experiments and more open-ended experiments are possible (Smith and Jones, 1986). For example, in studying solubilities, instead of memorizing tables or rules, students mix various reagents and generate their own table of aqueous solubilities of common salts.

Third, use of the learning centre relieves overcrowding in the laboratory (Jones and Smith, 1990). Lab instructors spend less time monitoring the lab and grading papers and more time working with students. Finally, controlled studies indicate increased learning in the learning centre compared to the 'wet lab' experience (Smith and Jones, 1989). However, the developers caution that the two experiences should be used in conjunction with each other. That is, students should experience the difficulties involved in setting up experiments in the laboratory and this experience is missing from the learning centre lessons.

The interactive exercises discussed in this chapter provide a variety of learning experiences for students. Among the activities associated with particular roles are experiencing the effects of interacting with others in a discrete situation; attempting to manage an adolescent character through difficult peer-related decisions; and working with others in learning about another historical period by taking a cross-country journey.

In contrast, problem-solving activities using simulated materials include group efforts to develop public policy for a particular region, troubleshooting complex equipment and conducting 'dry lab' experiments in chemistry. Each of these exercises provides learners experience with a unique dimension of problem-solving.

REFERENCES

Barlow, S L (1990) 'Interactive videodisc: TIP-DART provides alternatives for youth', *Instruction Delivery Systems*, **4**, 1, 15–18.

Clark, H L (1988) 'Air Force likes training on a "silver platter"', *Instruction Delivery Systems*, **2**, 4, 32–3.

Dalton, R, Minshull, R, Robinson, R and Garlick, J (1972) *Simulation Games in Geography*, London: Macmillan.

Dewey, J (1916) Democracy and Education, New York: Macmillan.

Jones, L and Smith, S (1990) 'Using interactive video courseware to teach laboratory science', *TechTrends*, **35**, 6, 22–4.

Leone, C J (1990) 'TARGET interactive project: A pilot evaluation study', *Instruction Delivery Systems*, **4**, 1, 16–17.

Martin, A (1985) 'Into the realm of microworlds: Simulation-database packages in the classroom', in van Ments, M and Hearnden, K (eds), *Effective Use of Games and Simulations*, 201–8, Loughborough: SAGSET, Loughborough University of Technology.

Scarcella, R and Stern, S L (1990) 'Reading, writing, and literature: Integrating language skills', in Crookall, D and Oxford, R L (eds), *Simulation, Gaming and Language Learning*, 119–24, New York: Newbury House.

Smith, S G and Jones, L L (1986) 'The video laboratory – a new element in teaching chemistry', *Perspectives in Computing*, **6**, 2, 20–26.

Smith, S G and Jones, L L (1989) 'Images, Imagination, and Chemical Reality', *Journal of Chemical Education*, **66**, 1, 8–11.

van Ments, M (1983) *The Effective Use of Role Play: A Handbook for Teachers and Trainers*, London: Kogan Page.

van Ments, M (1984) 'Using role-play effectively', in Jaques, D and Tipper, E (eds) *Learning for the Future With Games and Simulations*, 71–9, Loughborough: SAGSET, Loughborough University of Technology.

13 Discussion

Ten of the chapters in this text have each discussed a particular type of experiential learning activity appropriate for the classroom. Each chapter describes the major characteristics of a particular type of interactive exercise and the basic requirements for both the design of new exercises and the evaluation of existing ones.

Some of the critical design issues, however, are applicable across the different categories of experiential learning activities. Briefly summarized, they are the role of competition; deep structure; reality of function; and the role of technology. In this chapter, each of these recurring issues is discussed from the broader perspective of comparing the different kinds of experiential activities with each other.

THE ROLE OF COMPETITION

Competition that leads to the designation of a winner or winners is the primary characteristic that sets games apart from simulations. The essence of a game is competition in a make-believe environment in which the players strive to become winners. Of importance in games is that the contingencies established by the rules do not transfer to real-world events. Going to jail in *Monopoly*, for example, does not imply a similar penalty outside the game context. The primary differences between academic games and games for entertainment only are 1) the application of curriculum-based knowledge and skills; 2) the elimination of chance as a basis for winning; and 3) the use of team rather than individual competition.

Simulations, in contrast, establish hypothetical situations in which participants undertake a functional role and experience the responsibilities and consequences associated with complex problem-solving related to the role. Of importance in designing credible simulations is that gaming characteristics are not inadvertently incorporated into these interactive exercises. In other words, playing to win at any cost is an appropriate game behaviour, but is inappropriate in a simulation. In a game, winning is the sole outcome; therefore, risking one's resources and the resources of others in order to win is both logical and legitimate.

Simulations, in contrast, are activities that involve multifaceted tasks or problems. As a result, both the processes set in motion by the activity and the outcomes are diverse. Participants typically execute a variety of strategies and skills and they experience a range of consequences that are both affective and cognitive. Thus, to direct one's efforts toward winning at any cost in a simulation is to seriously distort, disrupt or destroy processes that lead to other anticipated outcomes. Such a level of competition, ie, winning at any cost, is unhealthy in a simulation.

Some curriculum areas maintain that learning is the goal, but the situations in use are those in which winning is the sole outcome that receives recognition. Thus, exercises are developed that generate negative behaviours. These behaviours do not contribute to greater insight or learning by the participants. Examples are the so-called 'business games' in which companies compete to acquire the greatest profits, the sole outcome that receives recognition.

Unlike the development of diagnostic simulations found in medical and dental schools, the development of data-management simulations in business colleges has yet to come to grips with the essential parameters for ensuring learning. The developmental effort in many business simulations focuses on the mathematical model that establishes the relationships among the selected variables and the surface characteristics of the exercise. In contrast, the emphasis in diagnostic simulations is on the processes by which correct diagnosis and management of the problem are accomplished. The goal for participants is to be both effective and efficient in their approach to the problem. Thus, the development of diagnostic simulations for prospective doctors and dentists begins with the construction of a map that indicates the variety of routes through the complex problem. In other words, development is guided by a profile of the variety of process decisions that are both possible and credible, along with supportive outcomes.

One purpose of simulations is to motivate the learner to become involved and to take appropriate action. However, to rely on competition in order to become a winner as a motivator is to ignore an important classroom characteristic. Specifically, students want to be successful. They are also more likely to try their best when those efforts will lead to some benefit. Therefore, any 'competition' in tactical-decision simulations should be between the participants and a pre-identified optimum model or course of action. The payoff for the students is threefold: 1) the opportunity to try their skills in a non-threatening environment; 2) receiving confirmation of their strengths both during the exercise and in a post-simulation conference; and 3) obtaining feedback and advice on ways to correct their weaknesses in a post-simulation consultation.

Sometimes unhealthy competition is inadvertently established in social simulations. One of two different circumstances typically precipitates the misuse of competition. First, designers may be unaware of other mechanisms for establishing a particular effect. On the other hand, they may be attempting to model the characteristics of a particular society and thereby stacking the deck against some participants so that they cannot possibly achieve their goals.

An example of the first circumstance is *Starpower*. As indicated in Chapter 10, hard feelings are likely to result that may transfer to the school or work setting. Instead of such an exercise, a single-agenda simulation should be developed in which all participants in the group experience the effects of a particular mechanism or process.

Similarly, efforts to mirror a particular society may result in the establishment of groups with unequal resources and differential mechanisms for maintaining or improving one's economic or social status. Some participants may experience frustration and/or humiliation, the learning outcome of which is questionable, because the more privileged groups will not comprehend the situation in the same way as the underprivileged group. Recall the reactions of Arthur Getis (1984) who participated as a poor farmer in *The Green Revolution Game*. He experienced jealousy of the more privileged families and humiliation when he had to ask them for assistance.

If the purpose of the simulation is for all participants to understand the mechanisms by which a particular society perpetuates itself and those mechanisms depend on a lack of social mobility, then a single-agenda simulation or an empathy/insight simulation should be designed. If participants can, through particular efforts, for example, work their way out of the poverty cycle, then a single-agenda simulation is appropriate. However, if the situation is one which does not respond to the efforts of the less-privileged groups, then an empathy/insight simulation is required (with all the cautions identified in Chapter 10).

DEEP STRUCTURE

One key factor that differentiates the various types of simulations is deep structure. First identified by van Ments (1984), deep structure is further defined as the nature of the interactions a) between participants and the situation, crisis, problem, task, etc., and/or b) among participants in the exercise (Gredler, 1990, p 329).

Two general issues are involved in determining the deep structure of a simulation:

- What behaviours are essential in addressing the focal task of the exercise?
- What participant behaviours are being reinforced during the simulation?

If the focal task requires the diagnosis of a complex problem or crisis or the interpretation and management of sets of data, then the simulation is an example of a tactical-decision exercise. The essential behaviours are the particular cognitive abilities referred to by Gagné (1977; 1985) as cognitive strategies. Also, of course, the participants must be exercising the responsibilities of a role that is instrumental and essential in addressing the focal task.

The behaviours that should receive reinforcement in tactical-decision simulations are data gathering, interpretation and management that addresses the basic problem. Note, however, that reinforcement is not synonymous with 'reward' (Skinner, 1953). Specifically, a reinforcing event is any event that strengthens a particular behaviour, ie, ensures that the behaviour will be repeated. Events that can strengthen behaviours include finding the right word to describe something, resolving a temporary confusion and having the opportunity to advance to the next stage of an activity (Skinner, 1968, p 380).

In tactical-decision simulations, receiving a key item of information for pursuing a particular clue can reinforce the analysis of the problem. In other words, success is a powerful reinforcer. Behaviours that are successful even in small ways, such as deciphering a particular clue to a problem, tend to be repeated. For this reason, simulations should be carefully reviewed and then observed during implementation to ensure that chance or inappropriate behaviours do not lead to even partial success. Also, in team exercises, behaviours that are designed to sabotage other teams should not be reinforced by success.

In contrast to tactical-decision simulations, the focal task in social-process simulations is some social or political agenda that influences human interactions in one or more ways. For example, participants may be striving to pass a particular law, to survive as a tribe in prehistoric times, to develop a plan for establishing an Arts Centre programme, or to escape from a frustrating or traumatic social experience. If properly designed, each of these simulations introduces interactions somewhat different from those that typically occur among the participants in their daily classroom activities. That is, participants may be required to negotiate for a particular platform, to communicate without a written language, to forge alliances among several compelling priorities, or to develop mechanisms as a group for undergoing a difficult or traumatic social experience.

In tactical-decision simulations, students can often achieve success in reaching their goals. That is, they execute well-developed deductive and organizational strategies. In contrast, achieving one's goals is highly problematic in social-process simulations. Participants in *Space Crash*, for example, may not survive.

Given the problematic nature of totally achieving one's goals in a social-process simulation, what potential reinforcements are routinely available in social-system and language skills simulations? Among them are positive feedback or support from other participants for one's actions or expressions of one's views, the resolution of conflict and reaching closure on an issue. Expressing oneself in a cogent or understandable way is also likely to be reinforcing because it indicates mastery of a particular concept and/or level of language use.

Because reinforcing events strengthen the behaviours that generate them, the rules established for social-system and language skills simulations are particularly important. They should be constructed so that sabotaging, blackmailing or otherwise derailing other groups or individuals is not followed by reinforcement. In other words, like data-management simulations, achieving a particular goal should not be reinforced by success if the strategy that was used involved overturning or sidetracking the system by illegal or illegitimate means.

The possibility of such an eventuality is one reason for not designing simulations in which unequal groups in terms of resources, social influence and access to power are established. Some privileged participants may further strengthen their position by collectively reducing the few opportunities or resources available to the others. Furthermore, the privileged groups, because they are far less likely to experience frustrating consequences than the underprivileged ones, do not undergo the same learning experience as the other participants.

Reinforcement of appropriate behaviours is the 'engine' that drives most simulations. In contrast, the lack of reinforcement for typical behaviours is the basis for empathy/insight simulation. Participants are placed in a situation in which their typical behaviours are ineffective and they are able to escape only through silent withdrawal. It is this characteristic of empathy/insight simulations – the total lack of reinforcement and the use of punishing consequences – that limits the use of such simulations to select adult groups whose subsequent decision-making may be influenced in a positive way. Thus, the deep structure of simulations that are traumatic experiences is the absence of reinforcement for typically executed behaviours. The best that the participant can hope for in traumatic situations is to escape punishment through withdrawal or to attempt to exercise one's autonomy through acting out (giggling, playing with the materials provided, putting one's head down on the desk and so on).

In other words, analysis of the deep structure of a simulation involves documenting the behaviours that occur consistently and the events or consequences that are maintaining those behaviours. In this way, flaws in the deep structure of a simulation may be identified and corrected.

REALITY OF FUNCTION

An important factor in differentiating simulations from other interactive exercises is reality of function. Although closely related to deep structure, reality of function is a different dimension in determining the nature of the interactive experience for the participant. As indicated in Chapter 1, reality of function occurs when participants accept their roles and fulfil their responsibilities seriously and to the best of their ability.

Three essential design requirements for establishing reality of function are 1) establishing bona fide roles for participants; 2) providing sufficient documentation so that participants can behave in a professional manner (Jones, 1987); and 3) providing behavioural contingencies in the simulation that support the conscientious execution of the participant's role. The third requirement, appropriate contingencies for designated behaviours, is also a component of the deep structure of the simulation. As indicated in the prior section, some simulations have flawed deep structures. Such simulations also lack reality of function because inappropriate participant behaviours are being reinforced.

Reality of function is one of the primary factors that differentiates simulations from both problem-solving activities with simulated materials and role-playing activities. Reality of function implies that participants execute responsibilities within a particular framework and the actions that they take at a later point in the simulation depend in part on the ways that the situation changed in response to their earlier actions and/or the earlier actions of others. Thus, simulations differ from problem-solving exercises with simulated materials because the participant is inside the context in the simulation and the complex problem or task becomes subtly redefined and reshaped in response to participant actions.

Role playing, on the other hand, is an open-ended situation. The participant is indeed inside the situation as in a simulation. However, the participant is free to incorporate his or her feelings, views, perceptions and definitions into the situation and is encouraged to do so. Thus, in a role-playing activity, the participant typically leaves his or her own creative stamp on the execution of the role. In contrast, in a simulation, although the participant has the freedom to execute different courses of action, redefining the role and other expressions of creativity that restructure the basic exercise are not permitted. Such actions would distort reality of function and turn the exercise in the direction of an acting or interpretative expression experience.

THE ROLE OF TECHNOLOGY

The development of the microcomputer and, more recently, computer-managed videodiscs, adds new dimensions to interactive learning. Of importance in the development of interactive exercises is that sound design guidelines govern the use of technology rather than the characteristics of the technology guiding the design.

At present, computers have been implemented either in a support role or as the deliverer of instruction. In the support role, a traditional use is the analysis of data. This application occurs most frequently in data-management simulations that are team exercises. Typically, financial analyses are completed for each round of decision-making for business and financial-management simulations.

An innovative use of microcomputers in the support role is in the development of microworlds. A movement-simulator provides a framework of travel and incident, and developed databases serve as information reservoirs related to the selected locale, time and roles in the scenario. The incidents in the scenario serve as catalysts for group activities in the classroom. Pauses incorporated into the scenario permit the groups to spend time investigating any of several topics related to the scenario.

The use of the microcomputer as the deliverer and manager of instruction (closed-structure simulations) is appropriate for some diagnostic and data-management simulations. The effectiveness of these exercises depends upon the ability of the design team to develop branching exercises with reality of function for the participants. That is, the problem situation, the variety of credible courses of action available to the participant and the credibility of the information provided in response to participant requests contribute to reality of function for the participant. Specifically, the simulation must mentally engage the participant in the assigned role and provide him or her with a credible decision-making experience.

Limited choices, dry feedback and linear (rather than branching) exercises obviously fail the test. A more serious problem in the computer-delivered experience is that of the variable-assignment exercise. As indicated in Chapter 7, the reliance on chance, inaccurate mathematical models and truncated decision-making result in exercises that lack educational applicability.

Another problem in the development of microcomputer exercises is that the technology has been used in an attempt to approximate a particular social setting and the interactive social processes that function in such settings. However, the purpose of social-process simulations is to provide new opportunities for individuals to participate in human interactions. Thus, the human interaction component is essential for reality of function, and this component is missing in all except a peripheral way.

The development of videodisc technology added the capability of providing still and moving pictures during instruction. When managed by the computer (Level III videodisc technology), branching computer-managed exercises may be developed. The incorporation of this technology can enhance reality of function for participants in closed-structure diagnostic and data-management simulations. This enhancement is accomplished by providing visual illustrations of data selection choices and consequences.

Videodisc technology, however, is not a substitute for human interactions. Therefore, the videodisc branching exercises developed for language learning should be categorized as problem-solving exercises with simulated materials. First, although the videodisc projects incorporate visual and auditory responses, the student must type in his or her questions and responses. Second, regardless of the skill of the programmer, the spontaneous adjustments that humans make to each other's speech patterns and accents cannot be replicated. Third, facial expressions and gestures that the student may use are omitted from the interactions.

In addition to problem-solving activities, another use of Level III videodisc technology lies in the development of role management exercises that address sensitive social issues. Students can identify with a peer in a difficult situation, choose alternatives and observe the effects in subsequent film events. The success of such exercises, like other pre-packaged learning activities, depends on the basic conception and the sequences of selected events and consequences (or script).

Simulations have evolved in a variety of ways since the early developments of the 1950s, as indicated by the breadth of the issues discussed in this chapter. They continue to be viable, interesting and absorbing ways for learners in any setting to explore new situations and to try new skills.

REFERENCES

Gagné, R (1977) *The Conditions of Learning*, (3rd edn), New York: Holt, Rinehart & Winston.

Gagné, R (1985) *The Conditions of Learning*, (4th edn), New York: Holt, Rinehart & Winston.

Getis, A (1984) 'Game review: *The Green Revolution Game*', *Simulation and Games*, **15**, 1, 119-20.

Gredler, M B (1990) 'Analysing deep structure in games and simulations', *Simulation/Games for Learning*, **20**, 3, 329-34.

Jones, K (1987) *Simulations: A Handbook for Teachers and Trainers*, London: Kogan Page.

Skinner, B F (1953) *Science and Human Behaviour*, New York: Macmillan.

Skinner, B F (1968) *The Technology of Teaching*, New York: Appleton.

van Ments, M (1984) 'Simulation and game structure', in Thatcher, D and Robinson, J (eds), *Business, Health and Nursing Education*, 51-8, Loughborough: SAGSET/Loughborough University of Technology.

Index

Notes

Notes

Notes

Notes

Notes

Notes

Notes

Notes

Notes